YOUR
HIDDEN
RICHES

Also by Janet Bray Attwood and Chris Attwood

*The Passion Test—The Effortless Path
to Discovering Your Life Purpose*

YOUR HIDDEN RICHES

UNLEASHING *the* POWER *of* RITUAL
to CREATE *a* LIFE
of MEANING *and* PURPOSE

Janet Bray Attwood
and Chris Attwood

with Sylva Dvorak, Ph.D.

HARMONY
BOOKS · NEW YORK

Library of Congress Cataloging-in-Publication Data
is available.

ISBN 978-0-385-34855-3
eBook ISBN 978-0-385-34856-0

PRINTED IN THE UNITED STATES OF AMERICA

Book design by Donna Sinisgalli
Jacket design by Jess Morphew

1   3   5   7   9   10   8   6   4   2

First Edition

CONTENTS

PART THREE

Your Greatest Riches

YOUR
HIDDEN
RICHES

INTRODUCTION: WHY RITUALS?

We—Janet and Chris—spend our days doing the most exciting work imaginable: showing people they possess a unique Life Design that runs through every part of their life. When this design is uncovered, things that seem random and accidental, or the product of bad luck and misfortune, suddenly make sense. This also applies to you. Instead of being the victim of circumstance, tossed around by forces you can't control, you can discover how fulfilling life is meant to be. Your Life Design makes everything click into place. Suddenly you are at the center of purpose and meaning. You matter in the most precious way possible.

This book will take you many steps deeper into your unique Life Design. It will help you reveal your hidden riches: the untapped potential that is disguised by the haphazard way most people live. Our approach is rooted in the most ancient traditions of our world, based on daily ceremonies, celebrations, and practices for deepening heart and mind—in short, a host of *rituals* that give your days shape and meaning. A lifetime is nothing but a series of days, and when you can uplift each one, you can discover heights you never thought possible.

But why rituals? The very word may bring up bad memories of empty rituals, like Thanksgiving dinner with family members who don't really want to be there, or saying grace as fast as possible to get down to the business of eating. Rituals imply formality, like a Japanese tea ceremony. Beautiful, but not suitable for the fast pace of modern life.

Contrast those moments with a formal wedding, at which ritual, ceremony, and celebration lay the foundation for an unforgettable experience. Janet recalls the day she married Chris in a small chapel: "I watched from the back of the hall as all our friends assembled in a mood of happy expectation. My six bridesmaids walked down the aisle, along with twelve little flower girls. Chris had to rush to get there on time, but there he stood, still slightly red and winded, waiting for his bride.

"It would be my turn in a minute, and suddenly I realized that I wasn't myself, not the self who had been frantically organizing this event and trying to make sure every detail was perfect. I'm a confident person who is used to performing in public. But I was trembling, on the verge of tears. There was something so profound in the atmosphere. It went beyond the joy of the ceremony. I almost felt like I was outside my body—and then I realized why. I was experiencing a sacrament. Organized religion hadn't been a part of my life for a long time, but at that moment, I peered into a kind of spiritual mystery: how the assembly of people gathered to join two souls creates a sacred space.

"I've never forgotten that little epiphany, and now, years later, I believe that creating a sacred space, not just in a chapel but in your own being, is one of life's most precious attainments."

Our intent is to help you unfold the richness of ritual that Janet glimpsed that day. We ask you to set aside your preconceptions. In reality, rituals have deep meaning that has been largely lost. Every day has the potential to unfold an epiphany, but few people know that they have this choice. In a moment we'll tell you an amazing story about one woman's experience of uncovering a layer of the mind she never dreamed existed. But first, a bit more about why this book is called *Your Hidden Riches.*

Your hidden potential is woven into the secret patterning of your life. The answers to your deepest questions and most cherished hopes aren't somewhere outside you. Life is the answer to life. You must connect with that part of you where these answers, your riches, lie.

What keeps people from finding their hidden riches? We've thought long and hard about that, and here is our conclusion. One of the happiest parts of anyone's life is connected to one of the saddest. The happy part is the dream you have of how your life is going to turn out. Beginning as children, we all assemble bits and pieces of an ideal picture, which is based on getting what we really want. To a six-year-old, what you really want is mostly within reach, because there is food and protection provided by your parents, friends and games, with lots of time to play. But if we fast-forward thirty years, often the dream has crumbled, and is now associated with sadness instead of hope.

Are you getting what you really want? Are you happy, fulfilled, and living life as you'd like it? If so, you have achieved something rare: You have found your Life Design, probably through much trial and error. Your destiny is being lived through work, relationships, and recreation. What could be more ideal? Life isn't really like a box of chocolates, despite what Forrest Gump's mother told him. It's rather like an enormous jigsaw puzzle that promises a beautiful finished picture, only the top of the box is blank. You are expected to assemble the pieces with no model to follow. To make the puzzle even harder, new pieces arrive every day.

It's actually quite amazing how well most people put together some kind of happy picture. But let's face reality. We all settle. Our ideal life has been switched out for something less, and even the happiest picture has its ragged edges, missing pieces, and hidden places where forgotten dreams have died.

In the United States, people hold on to an image of total freedom, the open road, and rebels without a cause. Living this way has become a goal for many young people the world over. Reality isn't like that. Beyond adolescent fantasies and romantic daydreams, real joy comes from knowing that you've built the best life possible, using your intelligence, creativity, and every fiber of your being.

As you'll soon read, rituals can be applied to small, everyday actions in order to make daily life rich and rewarding. Rituals can also be formal ceremonies that transform, connecting you to deep meaning in every aspect of your life, and may even change your entire life's direction. (We've gathered a rich collection of both everyday and ceremonial rituals to support your exploration of this remarkable world at www.thehiddenriches.com.)

So how are your hidden riches revealed? First, by knowing that they exist. Second, by bringing your mind to a deeper level of attention. Third, by channeling your life energy in new directions. We'll show you how to do all three, using rituals as the key, since they provide a natural route to a deeper reality, one that already exists within you. Attention is really the main focus, because all day, every day, you place your attention on one thing after another. If your attention is distracted, overwhelmed, stressed, and worried, then your daily life is being pulled this way and that by outside influences. For many people, just getting through the day is a form of barely organized chaos.

But if your attention is clear, open, relaxed, and fully present, everything changes. You see what is most important and meaningful to you, and you go for it. Rituals focus attention in a very practical way, as we will show in Part Two, where specific rituals are tailored to the major needs we all share. They are:

Relationships: Attracting your ideal partner and forming a loving bond between you.

Health, diet, and beauty: Bringing your body into harmony at every level so that it becomes your strongest ally in reaching a state of optimal well-being.

Money and wealth: Matching your inner riches with external abundance.

Ceremonial rituals: Creating a sacred space and entering it for healing and renewal.

Family: Bringing parents and children into a closer circle of security, understanding, and love.

All of these areas are expressions of your Life Design and when you are fully aligned with your Life Design, they create what we call "enlightened wealth." These are areas where fulfillment is meant to come naturally and in rich measure. We know you don't identify a higher state of fulfillment with rituals—not yet, at least—but that's been their purpose for thousands of years. Rituals work by organizing your attention in a new and better way.

To give you a sense of what's possible as you dive into the world of ritual, allow us to introduce Lynne Twist. For twenty years Lynne had been working tirelessly to end world hunger as chief fund-raiser for the Hunger Project. She had worked side by side with Mother Teresa, Nelson Mandela, and Archbishop Desmond Tutu; she trained thousands of volunteers. She had traveled throughout Africa and Asia, working with those most in need.

In 1995 Lynne got a call from one of her largest donors. He had a pet project he wanted her to help him with. When large donors call, fund-raisers listen. Lynne found herself on a flight to South America, where this client's work was under way. There she was joined by John Perkins, a longtime colleague and best-selling author of *Confessions of an Economic Hit Man.*

Nothing she had done prepared her for what lay ahead.

One evening Lynne and John were invited to join a small group in an ancient ceremony. Sitting around a bonfire, they and the group were led by a Mayan shaman, who instructed each person to "enter your dream" as he drummed. Expecting nothing to happen, Lynne did her best to follow his instruction. Suddenly she was transported into the body of a huge bird swooping and soaring over the jungle below.

"I didn't experience the dream of a bird," she recalls with excitement years after this occurred. "I *was* the bird. I could see the trees below and feel the wind in my wings." How could this be?

She surrendered to the experience, and as she continued to fly, she began to see faces rising from the jungle. They were strong faces, the faces of an ancient people painted in dramatic patterns that were not easily forgotten. Lynne has no precise idea how long her experience lasted, but when she felt herself return to her human body, she was deeply shaken.

"All of us sitting around the fire started relating our experiences. Each person had been transformed into some kind of animal—a jaguar, snake, or bird. The shaman explained that these were our spirit guides, and through these guides we could receive messages."

As it turned out, among the whole group, only Lynne and her colleague, John Perkins, shared the same experience of flying high over the jungle as a huge bird. John had also seen the painted faces that haunted Lynne after the ceremony. A few days later, she left for Africa to attend an important board meeting. She got caught up in new events, and they shoved aside the memory of her strange ritual experience.

She entered the boardroom and sat down with her papers. Looking around, she saw familiar faces, until, shockingly, the men began to assume exactly the same geometrical, orange painted designs she had seen in her "dream." Shaken, Lynne hastily excused herself from the meeting and went to the ladies' room, trying to make sense of what was happening to her. Still agitated, she quickly finished up her work in Africa and boarded a plane back to San Francisco; her husband, Bill; and the familiar hustle and bustle of city life.

But her visions wouldn't leave her alone. The painted designs reappeared, this time on the faces of the male cabin crew and other passengers. Lynne squeezed her eyes tight shut, praying this was nothing more than temporary burnout from a hectic work schedule that had consumed her for years. Nonetheless, when she got off the plane in California, she wasted no time phoning John, but he was traveling in South America, so she had to impatiently wait for two weeks until he returned.

When she finally reached him, the first thing he said was, "You're seeing them, too, aren't you?" The silence between them was the only confirmation both of them needed. While Lynne was in Africa, John had been trying to piece together what was happening. In his research he had already identified the distinctive facial designs as belonging to the Achuar people, an indigenous tribe in Ecuador who had little interaction with the modern world.

"They are trying to make contact with us, Lynne. We need to take a trip to Ecuador."

A trek was organized to a remote area deep in the Ecuadoran jungle where contact was made with the Achuar, a remote tribe who confirmed something astonishing.

"It was their intent," Lynne says, "to find a few souls whose hearts were open enough to receive the invitation they were sending. Oil companies were encroaching on their ancestral land, destroying everything in their path."

The only way the Achuar could contact the outside world was through spirit messages. They recounted for their visitors the prophecy of the Eagle and the Condor. "It was a powerful prophecy," Lynne says with feeling. "The Eagle represents the people of the world who have used their intellect to create modern technological advances, bringing themselves great wealth. But in the process, the people of the Eagle have become disconnected from the heart and the deeper spiritual values that sustain life.

"By contrast, the Condor represents the indigenous peoples of the world who have used traditional wisdom to keep their connection to values of the heart. Their reward isn't money but the riches of a powerful spiritual life. A life so powerful, it can send visions to someone far away, like John and me."

Lynne was deeply moved hearing the Achuar tell the rest. The prophecy predicted that at this time in history, the peoples of the Eagle and the people of the Condor must come together to ensure the survival of humankind.

"Part of this I already believed, that the so-called civilized world must protect indigenous people and reach out to them for the wisdom we've lost. But the Achuar told us something else: It is equally critical that the people of the Eagle awaken from their 'dream.'"

Lynne's experience, which emerged as she participated in a ritual, led to her resigning from the Hunger Project and changing the entire direction of her life as she, her husband, and their colleagues joined with the Achuar to found the Pachamama Alliance. This unusual partnership has led to saving over ten million acres of

Amazon rain forest from destruction and training more than three thousand facilitators to lead the Awakening the Dreamer symposia.

The warning described by the Achuar has been echoed by representatives of the oldest civilizations on our planet, from the Aborigines of Australia and New Zealand to the North American Anishinabe and other tribes to the spiritual teachers of the Vedic tradition in India and Nepal. They all convey the same message: Our world is at a turning point. Those of us in the developed world must find ways to reconnect with the spiritual dimension and interconnectedness of all aspects of life if we are to continue to thrive.

Yet the world is just a reflection of each of us. If you have had the feeling your life is at a turning point, that there is some important element missing that is essential to your happiness and sense of purpose, then you are not alone.

In Lynne's remarkable story there is a lesson for all of us. The essence of a meaningful life lies in reconnecting with the unseen spiritual forces all of us have access to. If you see yourself as only a single isolated part, you will never realize the whole. What holds true for the planet holds true for each individual—in other words, you and me. We aren't trapped in the comings and goings of the everyday world. Something rich and mysterious lies beneath the surface. Ritual is the time-honored way to reach that hidden treasure.

Our first book, *The Passion Test* (www.thepassiontest.com), was gratifying because so many readers said that it opened their eyes to the simple fact that life could be passionate, not just in romance but in the pursuit of their own personal vision. This new book focuses on the nitty-gritty, the daily rituals that bring out your best self and allow it to flourish.

We will show you, step by step, a way to assemble life's jigsaw puzzle. There is a design to your life. You were born with it. Uncovering your unique role and purpose in the world lies in uncovering that Life Design.

Our world is at a turning point. It needs you doing what you came here to do. When you achieve that, you will be living your ideal life, reaping the inner riches that are your birthright.

Part One

RITUALS *and* *your* IDEAL LIFE

A VISION OF FULFILLMENT

Rituals are tools to access your hidden riches. They can take you to the heart of your problems as well as to the heart of their solutions. This may be a new message for many of you, yet one of the purposes rituals have served for centuries is healing. They also served as the sacred connection to a higher reality. Why should you take such a journey yourself?

Rituals are all about reconnecting. When mind, body, and spirit are truly connected,

You feel more energetic.
You feel centered and powerful.
You are in the flow.
You emanate a glow, inside and out.

When you are connected, your life energy doesn't flow aimlessly like a river overflowing its banks. It's not like a jolt of electricity or a super-energy drink loaded with caffeine. Life force is integrating; it infuses the body and mind with exactly the right amount of energy to create flow, so that you are "in the zone" when doing what matters most to you. It guides your life when you are attuned to it and leads you on the path to fulfill your unique and special purpose for being alive. A vision of these energies is vitally important. In ancient India they were called *shakti*. In the Chinese tradition they were referred to as *chi,* and they go by other names in other ancient traditions around the world. Specific rituals were performed to increase these energies.

The words "shakti" or "chi" may sound esoteric, but what really matters is that everyone was born with it—you can see how vital, happy, curious, and vibrant a baby is. By contrast, when a grown-up feels dull, lethargic, anxious, or depressed, their life force is at low ebb. It only makes sense that maximizing your vital energy will improve your life.

Our aim is to modernize this ancient vision. The rituals that originated in ancient cultures can be adapted to our lives today. They are all about reconnection. When you are fully connected in mind, body, and spirit, you will be whole. This is our model of the ideal life.

THE DESIGN OF YOUR LIFE

If you look around, you can easily tell which person is leading a life with high fulfillment and performance. How? It's a state all of us would like to be in. Performance psychologists like Jim Loehr spend their careers helping multinational companies and Olympians connect with this life-force energy, creating breakthroughs, triumphing over crippling challenges, and achieving unusual success—all with the help of conscious, positive, consistent rituals. You can fashion the same kind of life for yourself.

It is the formal structure of ritual that allows participants to connect with the deepest aspect of their own inner nature. Look at the yoga movement, based in ancient ritual yet adapted to modern life to create connection among body, mind, and spirit. Or consider pilgrimages of the kind depicted in the popular movie *The Way,* which is about the famous pilgrimage route in Spain, Camino de

Santiago. The lead character, played by Martin Sheen, discovers that making a pilgrimage isn't solely about the holy place at the end. It's about finding yourself, connecting with your inner peace, and hopefully touching a sacred place inside you.

These are a few examples, but there's a much larger design that rituals fit into. Imagine if there was a built-in structure to your life that, when you align with it, will automatically create every day the experience of flow, ease, peace, and success. Imagine this as a structure that connects you with your unique purpose and role, immersed in a sense of belonging, at peace with yourself and the world. We call this structure your Life Design.

It's no accident that you love the things you love. What you are drawn to, what you are passionate about, what you are good at, are all part of the unique design of your life. When you are aligned with the design, you feel joyful, fulfilled, and purposeful. When you are out of alignment, you start to get unhappy, to suffer and become miserable. This discomfort is a sign that your life is off track from fulfilling your unique purpose. Something needs adjustment.

Through the life energy that sustains you, your Life Design is constantly unfolding within every cell of your body and every part of your being. Every cell is structured in a dynamic way, bubbling with thousands of chemical reactions per second. It's not a static structure like a blueprint or the schematics of a computer chip.

Because the structure of a cell is dynamic, it can respond to every change in the body—how much you've just eaten, how well you slept, whether your mood is elated or depressed. There's a tiny energy shift in every cell that reacts to these changes. Thus, every cell displays the perfect balance between order and spontaneity.

The same should be true in your life as a whole. Everyone knows the famous elevator scene in *Jerry Maguire* when Tom Cruise turns to a hopelessly smitten Renée Zellweger and says, "You. Complete.

Me." (Really? Tom Cruise looks like a guy who only needs some cool shades and a Maserati to be complete.) How is life made complete? By love, certainly, but also by investing in the things your hidden riches want to express. If every cell in your body yearns for something, that thing will make you complete. You were designed that way biologically.

Your cells thrive by exquisitely controlling the flow of energy that they use, extracted from the air and food they take in. In ancient wisdom traditions, the use of vital energy was carefully mapped out on every level. This provided an objective way to understand why

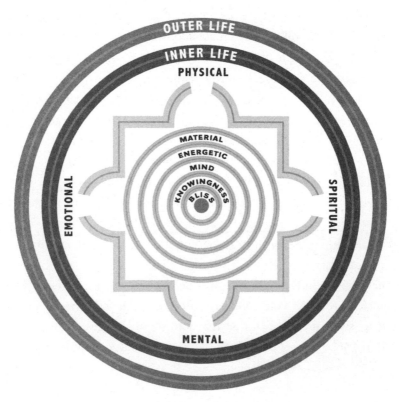

Model of Your Life Design

being aligned with one's life energy produced an optimal flow while being out of alignment produced struggle. The infinite potential at the center of every life was expressed through five levels, from the most subtle to the most physical.

From your transcendent center, or spiritual core, the infinite potential that exists there radiates out through five layers. Life energy transforms into new forms before finally flowing through what are traditionally called "the four gates" of physical, mental, emotional, and spiritual expression. All of this activity represents your inner life. You also lead an outer life, as represented by the ring that would encompass your social role and the appearance you give to others. Even those who know you best can't be fully aware of your inner life, and yet when you uncover your Life Design, inner and outer begin to match much more closely. There is no question of wearing a mask or assuming a public persona that is far from the real you.

The five layers through which the potential of your life expresses itself are:

The level of Bliss—This is the place from which the joy, the aliveness, the pure delight of being alive arise. Shakti flows from this invisible source.

The level of Knowingness—This is the part of you that can "feel" whether something is right or not without having to think it through. It is from here that intuition arises.

The level of Mind—This includes both thoughts and emotions and is where many of us stumble. When our thoughts and emotions are self-destructive, they block access to the levels of bliss and knowingness.

The level of the Energetic—It is the energetic level that attracts or repels. Ever meet someone and feel instantly attracted, or instantly repelled? You're responding to the energetic field that person is projecting. When someone is dark and depressed, you feel it. When people are loving and happy, you feel that as well.

The level of the Material Form—This is the physical expression of the previous levels. You will be able to see distortion in a person's Life Design by their physical condition. When people are well-aligned, they look vibrant, healthy, and happy.

When you are aligned with your Life Design, the two outer rings—one representing your Inner Life, the other your Outer Life—are perfectly symmetrical. Now we have a template for the ideal life. The laws of nature and the organizing power of your life force are structured within your transcendent center. Depending on your spiritual tradition, you may refer to this transcendent center as God, Allah, Jehovah, or Brahman, but we feel more comfortable using a value-neutral term: the source of infinite potential. The flow of energy that begins here travels and transforms into body, mind, emotions, and on through every level. Since this flow is natural and effortless, the ancient seers affirmed that life as a whole can be effortless.

This is such a sweeping claim that we need to unfold it in detail. We want to show that the key to turning struggle into ease, which includes every aspect of your life, is a set of rituals that reconnect you to the flow of your life energy. Let's consider exactly what that means.

WHY IS LIFE SUCH A STRUGGLE?

You may agree with the saying that everything happens for a reason, but do you actually see the reason behind the things that happen to you? From the first shock of having a beloved pet die when you were five to hearing your parents fighting behind a closed bedroom door, from standing by helplessly when a family member contracts cancer to watching a grandparent suffer from Alzheimer's, there are random traumas you have no control over. They don't seem to happen for any reason at all. To get anywhere in life requires personal power and inner strength that enable you to weather the storms.

This brings us directly to the mind. Imagine a huge warehouse whose doors are open. You step inside and look around. The space is empty, and in the dim lighting it seems to run on forever. The warehouse is so vast that anything and everything could be stored inside it.

This warehouse is your mind. The vast space waiting to be filled is your potential. No one told us as kids that filling this warehouse isn't voluntary—it's a requirement for every single person. Every experience, good or bad, from the moment of birth, has been adding to your mind. Now that you're an adult, you've gone a long way toward filling your mind with thoughts, feelings, memories, and all kinds of things. Nobody fills the mind in exactly the same way.

The most fortunate, happy, and successful people have discovered a secret about the mind. For these people, the mind isn't just a warehouse for random thoughts and feelings, impulses and desires. It's a place of hidden riches. All the love you will experience in your whole life—past, present, and future—is experienced here. Your hopes will be fulfilled here. Joy is here in abundance, once you know how to uncover it. The most valuable thing anyone can learn is how to find these hidden riches.

Failing to uncover these riches results in a life marked by disorder and confusion. Many people have turned the warehouse into a teenager's bedroom. Everything's a jumble. The floor is littered with whatever got picked up and tossed back down. The walls are cluttered with posters, stickers, perhaps a stolen stop sign, or sports logos. A teenager enjoys the luxury of a disorganized bedroom because his mother will usually get exasperated enough to come in and straighten out the mess. Unfortunately, if you keep filling your mind this way, no one is around to straighten out the jumble for you.

Your first reaction will probably be, "My mind's not like that." But we know lots of people who live their lives hoping to find success and fulfillment, yet who have no idea that their inner world is keeping them from reaching their goal. They have developed the habits of a disorganized mind, and the evidence can be seen in their typical day.

There's never enough time to get everything done.
Accidents and distractions crop up unexpectedly, pulling them this way and that.
At work and at home there's too much random activity.
Stress mounts up.
Deadlines keep pressing down on them.
Other people constantly drain their time and energy.

If you recognize this picture, it's not the outside people and events that are robbing you of your hidden riches. Your riches are getting lost in mental clutter, like a wedding ring dropped in a patch of weeds. It's hard for most people to see this. They work incredibly hard to get external rewards like money, the right job, a beautiful home. But despite the best planning and motivation, they feel frustrated. Too much of their inner potential has gone wasted or undiscovered.

This makes us think of Jonathan, now in his mid-forties, who followed his vision of being a self-made success. Jonathan knew as a teenager that he was a born salesman. He could talk to anyone. His outgoing personality quickly lowered social barriers, and he had tons of enthusiasm for any project he started.

And he started a lot. His mind was always whirling with the next bright idea. Having skipped college to start selling land in Florida, he quickly became restless. As much as his co-workers and bosses liked him, Jonathan gained a reputation for not following through. Contracts bored him, and so did seeing to all the nitpicking details of punch sheets and the complaints of renters. He moved on—to land sales in Colorado, car sales in California, then back to real estate. His restlessness ended only when he settled down with Karen, a loving wife.

A good period followed, in which Jonathan was able to start his own boat business, with a dream of one day selling yachts. "If you're a born salesman," he told his friends, "try and sell the biggest-ticket item you can. It's no harder than selling used VWs." But with all this enthusiasm and personal gifts, Jonathan never made his dreams come true. The telltale signs were always there:

He was impulsive, always following the next bright idea.
He hated being tied down to an orderly routine.
He left follow-through to others.
His financial affairs were always a mess, leading to money
    shortages and tax problems.

Above all, Jonathan's life didn't teach him any valuable lessons on which he could build a better future. Now divorced and falling back on low-level sales jobs, Jonathan is an example no one wants to imitate. But we feel a lot of sympathy for him, because millions of people are victims of mental messiness, lack of impulse control, and the inability to really develop their natural gifts.

In many cases this is a result of failing to discover and understand their own genius (yes, we all have genius) embedded in their Life Design. Discovering that genius allows you to connect with and partner with others whose genius is complementary, so that each of you is able to focus on your strengths—just as we (Janet and Chris) have done.

The things that block success and fulfillment aren't a mystery (although it feels like one when you're inside the chaos). Fulfilling your potential happens in the present. Here and now you must meet daily challenges, find solutions, and move forward. That's where the benefit of rituals begins, at the practical level.

SMALL RITUALS, BIG RESULTS

You already have your own personal rituals, small repeated routines that work for you. When the star NFL quarterback Tim Tebow knelt in prayer before a game, his ritual reconnected him to God and dedicated his playing to a higher power. When champion golfer Phil Mickelson closes his eyes and visualizes how he will play the next hole, his ritual focuses his mind in order to get the results he wants.

We were fascinated by a May 2013 article in *Scientific American* titled "Why Rituals Work." The authors note that personal rituals, "the symbolic behaviors we perform before, during, and after a meaningful event, are surprisingly ubiquitous, across culture and time." On the surface, the ritual can seem irrational, as in this example:

> I pound my feet strongly on the ground several times, I take several deep breaths, and I "shake" my body to remove any negative energies. I do this often before going to work, going

into meetings, and at the front door before entering my house after a long day.

We may keep it to ourselves, but most of us resort to some similar small rituals, and yet it would surprise us to hear that researchers have been examining the real benefits of personal rituals, which turn out to be quite rational. "Even simple rituals can be extremely effective. Rituals performed after experiencing losses—from loved ones to lotteries—do alleviate grief, and rituals performed before high-pressure tasks—like singing in public—do in fact reduce anxiety and increase people's confidence."

Before you assume that this must be a matter of faith, here's a surprising point: "Rituals appear to benefit even people who claim not to believe that rituals work." To back up these conclusions, the article cites an experiment in sports performance. Some subjects were given a "lucky golf ball" while others received an ordinary golf ball. When they were asked to perform a golf skill, the ones with the "lucky" golf ball did better, thanks to enhanced confidence. Performance also increased if the researcher merely told one group, "I'll keep my fingers crossed for you."

Is there a cause-and-effect connection between seemingly superstitious rituals and better outcomes? The authors of the article, who are professors and social behaviorists at Harvard Business School, leave this as an open question. But they conclude that rituals work, especially in situations where someone feels anxious or insecure. "Despite the absence of a direct causal connection between the ritual and the desired outcome, performing rituals with the intention of producing a certain result appears to be sufficient for that result to come true." Remember the key words "intention" and "desired result." They are going to play a huge part in this book.

Some of these private rituals are so valuable that they can make a difference out of all proportion to their size. Here's an example, given to us by a self-made millionaire who is a model of efficiency. His ritual isn't superstitious but highly rational, a comfortable place to begin. "I look at everything that happens to me in three ways. If I can answer a question or solve a problem in less than two minutes, I do it immediately. If the question or problem takes longer, it goes into two boxes. The first box holds the things I can resolve today or tomorrow. The second box holds everything else, the long-range things. It's a simple system, but you'd be amazed how well it has served me over the years."

This small ritual is actually quite brilliant once you look at the alternative. We've all had days when a thousand things needed doing. The first thing might be a task that takes an hour or more, such as paying the monthly bills. You get started, but right in the middle the mail arrives. There's an overdraft notice from the bank, which is surprising and alarming. Anxiously you run after this problem just as the kids come in and say they're hungry. While trying to get them fed, the phone rings and a friend wants to know when she can come over to talk about the charity bake sale.

The ritual our millionaire friend follows won't solve the whole mess, but consider its application here: You don't start paying the bills because that takes too long. It gets put in the box for things to do today or tomorrow. Fixing a snack for the kids takes about two minutes, so you do it in advance. The bank notice should take less than five minutes on the phone, so you address it next. When your friend calls about the charity event, you put that in the second box, for things that need long-range planning. You don't waste today's precious time when you are not in the right place for dealing with a long-range activity.

Highly successful people have discovered such time- and labor-saving rituals. They apply them every day, and thus they feel in control of their hectic, busy lives. Even better, they enjoy a platform of inner calm from knowing that distractions, chaos, and stress don't have the upper hand. (What's happening would be very clear to an ancient sage: Successful people are aligned with their Life Design. The modern twist is that we give our attention to externals first, while the ancients began with their inner world.)

Incorporating rituals into your life is very personal. There are three major areas where rituals can greatly benefit you.

The first is *time* and how you manage it.
The second is *energy* and how you expend it.
The third is *thought* and how you organize it.

A useful ritual improves at least one of these three things—and hopefully more than one. When you go to the check-in counter at the airport, you stand in line, wait your turn, and talk to the agent once you get to the front of the line. This may not seem to be a ritual to you, but visit a country where people don't form a line but instead clump together, each pushing and shoving to get to the front (we won't mention names, but we've been caught in such places).

The ritual of lining up saves time, energy, and thought. It seems obvious that it takes more time and energy to fight your way through a mob than to line up. But how is thought saved? The answer is that you don't have to worry about clawing your way to the front or plan ahead for the chaos or risk missing your flight, which would lead to spending thought and energy on all kinds of backup plans.

All effective rituals eventually come down to using your mind in a better way. But let's consider time and energy first.

Goal 1: Time At first glance time seems objective, the ticking of minutes and hours on the clock. But there is a subjective dimension, too. When Einstein was asked what his theory of relativity meant, where time can speed up or slow down, he made the famous remark that time goes by fast when you are with your sweetheart but very slowly when you are in the dentist chair. In other words, from a subjective viewpoint, time can drag or fly by. It can feel empty and lonely or rich and welcoming. Most of us are not very conscious about time. In surveys, parents tell pollsters that they have less and less family time, what with the increased demands on their schedule. But when actual measurements are taken, it turns out that families have more free time to spend together than in the past, on average over two hours a day. The subjective sense of being crowded, rushed, and pressured overshadows what the clock says.

Happiness is closely associated with how time is organized. For example, psychologists have found that the happiest people are those who spend at least one to two hours a day in meaningful contact with close friends and family members, by either talking, e-mailing, or texting. The important thing overall is *human* time.

You can assess this for yourself by taking a quiz on maximizing your time.

How Are You Spending Your Time?

Looking at a typical day in the past two weeks, how do the following ten statements apply to you?

☐ Usually ☐ Sometimes ☐ Rarely I have enough time to finish all my work.

☐ Usually ☐ Sometimes ☐ Rarely I don't feel stressed by deadlines.

☐ Usually ☐ Sometimes ☐ Rarely I feel in control of my schedule.

☐ Usually	☐ Sometimes	☐ Rarely	I leave some downtime to relax and unwind.
☐ Usually	☐ Sometimes	☐ Rarely	I take breaks between the busy parts of my schedule.
☐ Usually	☐ Sometimes	☐ Rarely	I plan for a little time to reflect or meditate.
☐ Usually	☐ Sometimes	☐ Rarely	I have time to play.
☐ Usually	☐ Sometimes	☐ Rarely	There's time to keep in touch with friends and family.
☐ Usually	☐ Sometimes	☐ Rarely	I have at least one activity that fulfills my long-range goals.
☐ Usually	☐ Sometimes	☐ Rarely	I do something for my personal development.
_____	_____	_____	
Usually	**Sometimes**	**Rarely**	**TOTAL SCORE**

A good score on this informal quiz would be having 5 to 10 "Usually" answers. A very good score would be at least 7 "Usually" answers. But many people would find themselves with a poor score, meaning 5 or more "Rarely" answers. A lot of "Sometimes" answers would put you in a gray area.

If you were living your ideal life, all your answers would be "Usually," and we believe that's possible. All time can be quality time. This includes downtime and time for meditation, when the qualities you are seeking are peace, calm, and ultimately inner wisdom. Rituals that improve how you use your time are many, as we will show you.

The key phrases that apply to time are:

Managing time well.

Finding time for each activity.

Alternating downtime and active time.

Making each time slot rewarding.

Making time for yourself in order to grow and develop.

Goal 2: Energy When they think about having more energy, most people begin with the physical side, in terms of eating a good breakfast, for example, and getting a good night's sleep. These are important things, and, medically speaking, the fact that in the United States half of the adult population don't get a satisfying eight hours of sleep at night is troubling. But the secret to maximizing energy is actually mental. Who works harder, someone who loves her work or someone who hates it? Which is more likely to put a spring in your step, going to a party or going to see your tax accountant?

The answer is obvious. Reaching your daily goals—and your long-range ones—requires the best use of your energy. This is a mind-body issue. For example, depression is considered a mood disorder that makes a person feel sad and hopeless. At the same time, however, depression drains energy. Sufferers feel exhausted to the point where the simplest household tasks feel impossible. In many cases, they are unable to reach deep sleep, or dream (REM) sleep, at night, and then wake up feeling fatigued rather than rested.

The brain is involved in everyone's energy level. Look again at the obstacles to success and fulfillment that we have touched upon already: stress, random daily intrusions, bad habits, anxiety, personal insecurity, aimlessness, lack of vision, the inability to settle down, resistance from others, distractions, and defective relationships. They all drain energy and they are all focused primarily in the mind.

Fortunately, there are mental connections that you can take advantage of for boosting your energy. Studies have found, for example, that workers will increase their productivity if they are given a pay raise, but they will boost it more if they are given attention and appreciation—and the effect will last longer, because a pay raise wears off after a few weeks or months. A young child who is consistently made to feel loved and worthy will generally be motivated for a lifetime.

Like the quiz for how you use your time, here's one related to energy. It will give you a snapshot of how many mental energy boosters you are taking advantage of. As you'll see, the major boosters of energy throughout the day are mental, as we've been proposing.

You can assess this for yourself by taking a quiz about maximizing your time.

How Are You Spending Your Energy?

Read the following ten sentences and circle the answer that best applies to a typical day in the past two weeks.

☐ Usually   ☐ Sometimes   ☐ Rarely   I enjoy my work.

☐ Usually   ☐ Sometimes   ☐ Rarely   I feel appreciated for what I do.

☐ Usually   ☐ Sometimes   ☐ Rarely   I feel respected and valued in my occupation.

☐ Usually   ☐ Sometimes   ☐ Rarely   I approach my work rested and alert every day.

☐ Usually   ☐ Sometimes   ☐ Rarely   I don't end my day exhausted. Often I feel energized, in fact.

☐ Usually   ☐ Sometimes   ☐ Rarely   I feel secure enough about money that it's not a source of worry.

Usually	Sometimes	Rarely	
☐ Usually	☐ Sometimes	☐ Rarely	I relate well to the people I work with or see every day.
☐ Usually	☐ Sometimes	☐ Rarely	I feel cheerful and optimistic.
☐ Usually	☐ Sometimes	☐ Rarely	I set meaningful goals and reach them.
☐ Usually	☐ Sometimes	☐ Rarely	I consider myself a success.
Usually	**Sometimes**	**Rarely**	TOTAL SCORE

A good score on this informal quiz would be 5 to 10 "Usually" answers. A very good score would be at least 7 "Usually" answers. But many people would find themselves with a poor score, meaning 5 or more "Rarely" answers. A lot of "Sometimes" answers would put you in a gray area.

Each item in the quiz boosts your energy if you can achieve it, from being cheerful and optimistic to setting worthy goals and reaching them. Achieving these energy boosters is crucial, with the added benefit that they increase happiness at the same time. Another big factor is managing a limited resource. We face every day with only a finite amount of energy.

For centuries, the expenditure of energy meant grinding physical labor that required every available ounce of biological energy available. As late as 1900, despite the invention of motorized farm equipment, 80 percent of the calories expended in farm work came from human muscles. Today the situation is reversed. Mental, not physical, energy comes first. Mental energy isn't measured in calories (although thinking does use calories). Instead of having energy sapped by physical demands—such as getting in the harvest before a looming thunderstorm—modern people live within flexible boundaries. They can organize how they spend their energy, but this poses its own problems. Inertia, disorganization, the frantic meeting of deadlines, bringing home work from the office, and other forms of wasted energy cry out for a better system.

Rituals that focus on energy are powerful tools, and all successful people have learned to harness them. Their day involves some key points for maximizing energy, with established habits that ensure that each one is attended to. The following are among the most important, as we'll show you throughout the book:

Boring and routine work is minimized.
Time is taken for rest and replenishing one's energy.
Energy-draining people are kept away.
Work is personally meaningful.
Exhaustion is avoided.
Mental alertness is maintained.

Goal 3: Mind Besides time and energy, there's a third area that rituals can help you with: thought. We are using the term to cover all mental activity. Whatever enters your mind is either contributing to success and fulfillment or detracting from it. Ever since the era of efficiency experts, who began to study work habits more than eighty years ago, the focus has been on productivity, which can be measured objectively. But thought is internal, private, and subjective. Only you can truly measure the experience you are having inside. A haphazard approach to one's inner world, which is how most people approach it, makes life a struggle. We speak from painful personal experience. One of the authors, Janet, had a difficult childhood, which offered little chance for happier prospects. By the time she was in her teens, she had been physically abused, had become strung out on drugs, and lived for a short time with the leader of the Oakland Hells Angels. Her young life was spinning out of control. In an existence where she once swallowed thirty-six tabs of LSD at once, she was holding on by her fingernails.

The turning point for Janet came from an unexpected source. In the midst of chaos, she learned to meditate. It was a leap from one lifestyle to almost the opposite. The kind of meditation she learned, TM or Transcendental Meditation®, had become widely popular in the West. It was non-religious, focusing on consciousness instead of on God. She had reason to worry that meditation might not even work for her, given her history of drug use and the emotional challenges she faced. She was reassured on these counts, and from the first time she practiced it, it made a difference. She experienced an inner journey to a deeper, quieter, more coherent part of her mind. She could feel layers of stress pouring off, and with such tangible results, the sharp contrast between one way of life and another was inescapable. For Janet, meditation was life-saving—what began as a doorway turned into a lifelong exploration. This book is just one fruit of her journey.

The discovery that your mind can be transformed is perhaps the most important discovery life can deliver. The image of a warehouse—where everything is effortlessly and spontaneously correctly inventoried, where nothing gets lost or misplaced, where the labeling system is easily understood so that any object can be retrieved instantly—is what we mean by a coherent mind. This can be the picture of your inner world. When it is, you actually have time to devote to your personal vision of what life should be. Your mind should be your best friend and strongest supporter. The following quiz will tell you how close you are to achieving that ideal.

You can assess this for yourself by taking a quiz about maximizing your mental processes.

How Well Is Your Mind Treating You?

Read the following ten sentences and circle the answer that best applies to a typical day in the past two weeks.

☐ Usually   ☐ Sometimes   ☐ Rarely   I basically have positive thoughts and feelings.

☐ Usually   ☐ Sometimes   ☐ Rarely   I am not pessimistic or depressed.

☐ Usually   ☐ Sometimes   ☐ Rarely   I am settled in my mind, not restless or discontented.

☐ Usually   ☐ Sometimes   ☐ Rarely   I feel free to express myself to others.

☐ Usually   ☐ Sometimes   ☐ Rarely   I have creative impulses and can follow up on them.

☐ Usually   ☐ Sometimes   ☐ Rarely   My memories give me pleasure, even though not all are positive.

☐ Usually   ☐ Sometimes   ☐ Rarely   I anticipate the future with hope and good expectations.

☐ Usually   ☐ Sometimes   ☐ Rarely   I feel safe and secure, not anxious or insecure.

☐ Usually   ☐ Sometimes   ☐ Rarely   I am tolerant of other people and their viewpoints.

☐ Usually   ☐ Sometimes   ☐ Rarely   I can easily tap into a level of my mind that is peaceful and calm.

_____   _____   _____
Usually   **Sometimes**   **Rarely**   TOTAL SCORE

A good score on this informal quiz would be 5 to 10 "Usually" answers. A very good score would be at least 7 "Usually" answers. But many people would find themselves with a poor score, meaning 5 or more "Rarely" answers. A lot of "Sometimes" answers would put you in a gray area.

Janet considers herself living proof that a person's self-rating on all of these important points can be dramatically improved. Compared to herself as a teenager, when she would have marked many with a Rarely, today she finds that Usually is her answer to every statement much of the time. The ideal of making your thoughts your best friend is within your grasp, too, as we will show in the following chapters.

People who have successfully attained an orderly mind are in the habit of reinforcing the life-enhancing aspects of thinking. The following points, which can be made stronger through daily rituals, are especially crucial:

Be thankful and express gratitude for the good things already in your life.

Acknowledge yourself and celebrate your small victories every day.

Bond with other people, seeing things from their perspective.

Stay centered.

Remain curious and open-minded.

Tap into deep peace and calm inside.

Release your imagination and other creative sources.

Be of service to someone else.

Solve at least one challenging problem.

THE SPIRITUAL DIMENSION

In your daily life you have found your own way to deal with time, energy, and mind. We dedicate this book to improving those ways. Yet even the most efficiently managed life can't be called a fulfilling one until you know what purpose it serves. Your Life Design will unfold your reason for being here and unlock the potential for a much higher level of fulfillment.

In a very general sense, that's what is meant by the spiritual side of life. Here rituals find their greatest meaning. The greatest riches anyone can find are spiritual, but they are also the most hidden. We are all heirs to the scientific revolution that turned thought into a rational process. The brain is now the ultimate smartphone combined with the ultimate personal computer. A strictly rational mind isn't completely true to life, however. It leaves out the search for meaning at a higher plane of existence.

Science can do without spirit, perhaps, but the everyday person feels empty and lonely if life is nothing but a collection of raw data assembled into facts. Here is one area where ritual still holds sway, through all manner of religious observations, prayer, and invocations of God. In our view, the ceremonial part of such rituals is beautiful and raises our spirits. But ritual has a bigger spiritual dimension. It can bring you closer to your soul. It can connect you to a higher power in the universe. It can allow you to tap into unknown resources of creativity and intelligence.

Earlier we touched upon how Janet's life was transformed by meditation. As a spiritual practice, meditation can unlock the mind's higher dimensions. At the very center of every Life Design is the transcendent, which means that the whole picture is upside down from our modern view, where the physical world dominates and the spiritual world is a faint shadow. For millions of people the transcendent world is probably an illusion—at best, they hope to go to heaven when they die, the only kind of transcendent reality they have ever heard about. But every Life Design begins with transcendence (and in many ancient traditions the physical world is seen as an illusion). In other words, bliss is basic to life.

In this book we don't want to get hung up on terms like "soul," "God," or "spirit"—we are happy with any terminology you feel comfortable with. Too much wrangling over God has clouded the fact that the spiritual dimension of life is natural; it exists within everyone as the deepest level of the self and emerges spontaneously in moments of joy, love, and creativity; in reverence for natural beauty; and awe before the infinite expanse of the universe.

Although we have left the spiritual dimension for last in this chapter, we feel that consciousness should come first in an ideal life. When you are aligned with your Life Design, a never-ending journey is mapped out for you. That's much better than experiencing a string of inspiring moments that have no real connection with one another. When you see that they are stepping-stones on your journey, it makes all the difference. Looking back, Janet can see that even her difficult years as a teenager were a stepping-stone; they offered such a powerful contrast to what she experienced in meditation that her commitment and passion were all the stronger.

The spiritual dimension, in other words, isn't just something that only religious people are interested in. The rituals that focus on spirituality deliver the following kinds of experiences:

You feel light, energetic, and free from burdens.
You walk around feeling at home in the world and at home in yourself.
You know that you are loved, and you can love in return.
You feel connected to a higher power.

Your life is full of meaning and purpose.
You feel at one with all that you experience.

These experiences aren't delivered in a package neatly tied with a ribbon when you reach the end of your journey. They appear along the way and get stronger as you make progress. Your brain gets trained to understand and value much subtler aspects of the mind, and thus you turn into the self that can live an ideal life.

The key words that apply to the spiritual dimension include the following:

Reverence
Bliss
Connection
Celebration
Appreciation
Surrender
Expansion
Devotion
Love

This book will delve into those practices that have proved over time to increase a person's state of fulfillment in every area. On the practical side, we will show you how to maximize your use of time, energy, and mind. On the spiritual side we will point you toward higher meaning and fulfillment. We won't be satisfied until your Life Design has been opened for you and for everyone else who yearns to make life better and better.

FOUNDATION RITUALS: GETTING INTO THE RHYTHM

This is what rituals are for . . .
to create a safe resting place
for our most complicated feelings of joy or trauma.

ELIZABETH GILBERT, *EAT, PRAY, LOVE*

We love Elizabeth Gilbert's inspiring and honest book *Eat, Pray, Love,* especially for a reason that applies to rituals. Her title tells the whole story of rituals in three words. Eating is a daily ritual that brings people together and creates an open space at the table. Praying is a ceremonial ritual for those who attend church or temple; it expresses a communal desire to be close to God. Love isn't a ritual but the fruit of the richest rituals: your life increases in the power to love and be loved.

If we all felt nourished by eating, praying, and loving, existence would be close to ideal—the rhythm of life would flow easily and from a deep source. To establish such a rhythm is the most basic change you can make right now. To show you how, we've constructed a set of foundation rituals for organizing your entire day seamlessly. But first let's talk about why it's important to care for yourself in the first place.

When you make time every day to take care of yourself, you also offer a reminder that you care *for* yourself. There's no need for a grand show of self-love. Small daily rituals bring you back to a basic relationship, which needs no words. You are the only one in this relationship, which sounds impossible. Doesn't it take two to tango? Of course, but a single human being is complex. Each of us plays many roles in life—at this moment you may be a worker, parent, caregiver, authority, lover, or citizen. Each role comes up as needed.

It's not automatic to fuse these separate roles into a single self. In fact, the tendency is to lose yourself in your roles. Hence, the harried mother of two young children who wonders if she's still attractive—the role of lover has somehow slipped away. The rituals of caring for yourself are a way of knowing that you are more than the roles you play.

Let's see where you are right now by taking a simple quiz.

ARE YOU CARING FOR YOURSELF?

How many of the following rituals, routines, or habits do you follow in your daily life? Looking at your normal day, put a check beside each one that applies to you.

- ☐ I acknowledge myself for a small (or large) victory every day, a success at meeting a problem or challenge.
- ☐ I have a regular time-out that is only for myself.
- ☐ I sit down and reflect on my day and how it's going.
- ☐ I give myself a gesture of appreciation.
- ☐ I connect for at least half an hour with someone close to me who really matters.
- ☐ I pray for comfort, peace, and guidance.
- ☐ I do something to nourish my soul, such as being of service for someone else, if only in a small way.

☐ I have a moment of reverence, whether for God, for someone who has departed, a cherished mentor, a saintly figure, or the traditions of my people.

☐ I take time to nourish my body with food that is good for me.

☐ I express love and appreciation for my own being.

Total _____

Looking at your score: All of the items on this list are good, so there is no poor score. You want as many of these good things as you can have. If you already do 6 to 10 of these things, you have a strong, caring attitude toward yourself. You take time to connect with others. You see your life as part of a bigger picture, one that you value and are proud to belong to. If you checked 1 to 5 things, you haven't paid as much attention to caring for yourself as you could. You are likely to be time-rushed, pressed by daily events that demand too much. It's likely that you have succumbed to the chaos of modern life.

So how can you make more time for self-care when you already feel a bit overwhelmed? That's where foundation rituals come in, as we'll now show.

FOUNDATION RITUALS

When you're building a house, you begin by creating a strong foundation. Foundation rituals provide the basis on which you can build the kind of life you choose to have. Everyday routines impact all three areas of life—time, energy, and mind—that need to be optimized, so we can't take them for granted. When you establish your own rhythm, you are freed up to focus on what really matters—

reconnecting with yourself and stepping out of the craziness at the same time.

Foundation rituals help you create a natural rhythm to your life that helps you maintain focus and attention over time. Just like the rhythm in music makes you tap your foot and want to sing along, when you use foundation rituals to create a rhythm for your life, you'll discover that life seems to go more effortlessly; the activities of your day become fun and energized rather than oppressive and draining.

We've constructed the following chart as a menu of choices. Our advice is to start with a few changes—the ones that feel most comfortable—and begin to feel the rhythm of your day as it gets more and more settled. Once the first changes have become automatic, add more. Rituals are never an end in themselves. Test each change by how free you feel to take care of yourself and pursue your daily goals.

Do the authors follow all the foundation rituals listed here? On a good day, yes. On a medium day, more than half. On a hectic day, as many as we can. That's why the menu looks so long. But don't roll your eyes. If our two-hour morning routine is simply impossible, incorporate a ritual or two that takes only a minute, or that you can do while taking a shower or shaving. We know you'll feel the benefit. There's a beauty and flow to an orderly life, which is what we want you to experience.

RITUAL PRACTICE

Daily Routine

Morning Menu

Choose among the following. Alter the times to fit your personal schedule:

6 a.m.: Rise—Waking up, take a minute or two to envision the day ahead. Think about what you want to accomplish. See yourself tapping into a reservoir of inner energy for each part of your day, and be positive in what you see for yourself, including how you will solve possible challenges.

Rising from your night's sleep, say to yourself, *"Thank you for this day. May I do good today and provide useful and appropriate service to each person I meet."*

6:00—6:30 a.m.: Showering and cleansing, saying, *"Thank you for this cleansing water to rinse away all my cares and tension."*

See yourself as renewed and refreshed. As you wash away the remains of yesterday from your skin, wash away any stains of held-on anxiety, anger, resentment, or other negativity.

6:40—6:50 a.m.: Yoga exercises or other light stretching. Before you begin, say:

"Thank you for allowing me to work and serve with health, energy, and vitality."

Or,

"Let me act for the good of all, expressing inner strength and grace."

6:50—7:00 a.m.: Sit quietly and gently follow your breath (or perform *pranayama,* the "alternate nostril breathing" exercises described on pages 78–79).

As you finish, say, *"Thank you for this breath. May I continue to enjoy the breath of life forever."*

7:00—7:30 a.m.: Meditate or pray in silence, using the technique of your choice to center yourself. Go inward, finding the most settled state of your mind.

7:30—8:10 a.m.: Practical time. Put together what you need for the upcoming day. Take a minimal amount of time to check the news and scan your e-mails. If it fits your schedule, take a walk to connect with nature or go for a run, or work out. The more you can do outside, the better.

8:10—8:30 a.m.: Breakfast. Don't rush or distract yourself. Taste your food; talk to each member of your family. Offer appreciation and encouragement to them as they set off on their own day.

Express appreciation for the food before you, either in the form of a prayer, a song, or a simple statement. It could sound something like, "Thank you for the abundance of this food, the love I feel for my family, and the grace that has brought us together in joy."

8:30—9:00 a.m.: Travel to work. Walk or bike if you can. Open yourself to the natural elements of sun, sky, wind, and the feel of a waking world. Say,

"Thank you for the ability to see, hear, touch, taste, and smell this world. I drink in the beauty of a new day."

9:00 a.m.—noon: As you begin your day, take a moment for yourself and say, *"Thank you for this work, that I may be of use to others. Let me perform my tasks with joy, creativity, and intelligence. May my contributions always be for the good of everyone."*

While at work, keep yourself connected and feeling good. Do some or all of the following:

Once an hour get up and walk around.

Talk on the phone, text, or e-mail someone who is close
to you. Talk about how you feel. Get interested in
what you say to each other.

Support and appreciate a co-worker.

Discuss a project that excites you with a colleague who is
equally excited.

Skip the gossip around the watercooler.

Take a break outside.

Sit with eyes closed for five minutes to center yourself.

Afternoon Menu

Choose among the following. Alter the times to fit your personal schedule:

Noon—1:00/1:30 p.m.: Midday pause, lunch. Beyond just eating lunch, design your midday pause to include nourishment for your heart and your spirit. Talk to people you value and cherish. Take a walk outside to refresh your spirit. Be sure to move and be active at least part of this time. You can also sit quietly and reflect on how the day is going, saying, *"Thank you for the fruits of this day. May it continue to get better and better."*

1:30—5:00 p.m.: Afternoon work—repeat the rituals of the morning work period.

5:00—5:30 p.m.: Travel home from work. Try to give this time the same interest as in your morning commute. At some point say, *"Thank you for this day, which has added to my being and my life. It will never come again. I appreciate it and release it."*

5:40—5:50 p.m.: Yoga exercises or gentle stretching. The purpose is to naturally release the tensions of a busy day, bringing your body into a relaxed, balanced state.

5:50—6:00 p.m.: Sitting quietly, repeat the gentle breathing exercise from the morning, along with the same words: *"Thank you for this breath. May I continue to enjoy the breath of life forever."*

Evening Menu

Choose among the following. Alter the times to fit your personal schedule:

6:00—6:30 p.m.: Meditation and/or prayer time, repeating your practice from the morning.

6:30—7:30 p.m.: Evening meal. The most important time for the whole family to sit down together, made even better if everyone helps prepare the food. Spend time paying attention to every family member's day. Offer encouragement and appreciation.

This is also a time to avoid the things that discourage families from having dinner together, such as complaining about your day, arguing over touchy subjects, offering unwanted advice, volunteering "constructive" criticism, sulking, and radiating silent disapproval.

Either share in the following blessing or say it to yourself: *"Thank you for everything that nourishes the mind, the body, and the spirit. May this meal be a celebration of all three."*

7:30—9:30 p.m.: Evening activities, which should be in the spirit of fun, recreation, and enjoyment. Pursue the projects you find most fulfilling. Without making the Internet, television, and video games bad, find a few alternatives that bring out your creativity and connect you to other people in real time.

9:30—10:00 p.m.: Prepare to retire. Slowing down your activity, mental and physical, before you go to bed encourages a good night's sleep. A stroll in the moonlight, a warm bath, a cup of herbal tea—choose a regular ritual that puts you in the proper framework.

> *10:00 p.m.*: Bedtime. To encourage sleep, have the room as dark and quiet as possible. Lie on your back for a moment, following your breath with eyes closed. As you relax, review your day. Reflect first on the positive things you achieved, then on the challenges you want to meet, and finally on any disappointments that could make your experience better next time. Give yourself permission to release them all, saying,
>
> *"Thank you for this precious day. Now that it is over, I send it back from where it came, with gratitude."*
>
> Finally, end the day by seeing everyone in your life you want to bless, one by one. Send your love to each one.
>
> Turn over and let the arms of sleep enfold you.

There is a thread running through the daily routine we've outlined above: gratitude. You can direct your gratitude to God, the universe, or life itself, depending on which feels meaningful to you. The point is to ground your day in a positive value that will then grow in your life.

A VITAL KEY—
CONSCIOUS INTENTION

To have any real benefit, everyday rituals must be conscious and intentional. This is what sets a meaningful ritual apart from an empty one.

Conscious means that you are applying your attention.
Intentional means that you have a goal or purpose in mind.

Putting these two things together creates a powerful effect. They keep you focused on the good instead of the anxious and irrelevant.

Consider the ritual of reviewing your day before you fall asleep at night. It is conscious because you are focusing your mind on remembering the important highs and lows of your day. It is intentional because you want to learn from your mistakes, appreciate your successes, and then move forward.

If you consistently followed this ritual, your whole life could change. You would be linking each day with the one to come. This forms a meaningful path of growth. You would wake up each morning with the secure knowledge that you are assembling your life based on lessons being learned every day. What could be more valuable? And it takes only a small everyday ritual to achieve big results.

Approach each foundation ritual in the spirit of becoming more conscious in your intentions. For example, how would your day change if, before getting out of bed, you lie there for a moment or two, setting your intention for that day, envisioning exactly what you want to accomplish?

Or as you're taking a shower, what if you took stock of the things you are grateful for that led you to this particular day? Or while brushing your teeth, instead of daydreaming or worrying, you thought about the things you appreciate about yourself? By making healthy choices part of your regular routine, you don't have to think much about them. In addition, creating regular, conscious intentions provides a structure and foundation that will help you weather the inevitable storms and slay the mental dragons that want to sabotage your happiness.

In this way rituals carry your intention throughout the day. Consider a composite person, Joe, who is a creature of habit. Every day begins with Joe's eating breakfast while keeping one eye on the morning news, grumbling to himself about how the world keeps going to hell in a handbasket.

At work he takes a coffee break at 10:30, spending most of the time trading gossip and embarrassing stories about other workers. He always takes time to stop in with a buddy who shares his political views, so that they can gripe together.

When he gets home he sits down in front of the evening news with a drink in his hand. As footage of the day's disasters unwinds, there is always more reason to feel that everything is getting worse. After dinner, when he listens to his wife's complaints and she listens to his, he falls asleep in the living room, watching a soccer game.

One could fairly say Joe leads a life full of empty rituals that hardly ever vary. He unconsciously repeats the same actions; his mind today is repeating the thoughts it had yesterday. To this, add the element of intent. Joe mostly doesn't have any. Instead of shaping his life, he drifts through it. What a terrible waste of the mind's potential, even though if we take an honest look, most of us would see a bit of Joe in ourselves—our days are lived by rote.

To get out of this trap and raise your life to a more fulfilling level, consider the following. Every hour of your day from morning to evening can be fulfilling in an easy, natural way. There's no need to go unconscious. All you need is a structure that shapes the day in a positive way. The first thing is to obey the natural cycles that govern your body—eat at regular times, get enough sleep, take time out to rest when you are being active. Medical science has validated over and over that the body's biorhythms cannot be ignored. Lack of sleep, for example, is connected with overeating, heart disease, depression, and fatigue. The buildup of stress hormones is accentuated when you are tired all the time.

Second comes the whole issue of stress, which all of us pay lip service to without actually following through. Stress is cumulative. It's like building a mountain by adding one pebble every day. Modern life has unavoidable stresses, beginning with the fast pace that we move at. But your body knows how to clear stress from the system if you give it a chance. Managing stress comes down to getting out of the way so that the mind-body system can return to a natural state of balance.

Third, the amount of time, energy, and thought available to you during a single day is limited. If you squander them, they are lost forever. Think of the stereotypical dad who works so hard that he has no time to watch his kids grow up. Ten years later, when he looks back and realizes what he's missed, time has slipped through his fingers. But time doesn't slip through in years and months. It slips through in minutes and seconds. If you face this fact, your best choice is to organize the basic needs of your day so that they can go on autopilot, leaving you free to use time in a meaningful and hopefully joyous way.

Consciousness and intention are the mind's most powerful tools.

It's a basic fact of psychology that "what you put your attention on grows stronger in your life." So why not set up your day to reinforce the healthiest choices and attitudes? You can transform your existing routine into everyday rituals without adding any more time to them, just by adding conscious intent.

MARCI'S STORY

The opening quote for this chapter was an excerpt from a longer passage from Elizabeth Gilbert. She is very eloquent about delicate balances.

> This is what rituals are for. We do spiritual ceremonies as human beings in order to create a safe resting place for our most complicated feelings of joy or trauma, so that we don't have to haul those feelings around with us forever, weighing us down.

In other words, ritual creates an inner sanctum or sanctuary. Gilbert goes on to expand on how necessary this is.

> We all need such places of ritual safekeeping. And I do believe that if your culture or tradition doesn't have the specific ritual you are craving, then you are absolutely permitted to make up a ceremony of your own devising, fixing your own broken-down emotional systems with all the do-it-yourself resourcefulness of a generous plumber/poet.

Everyone can fix—or at least begin to heal—their broken-down emotions. Who doesn't have this need? Modern society has created a vacancy here as traditions have died out. Fortunate are the people who grow up in families where the everyday rituals of life aren't empty but filled with happy associations. They form a solid foundation for deepening the value of ritual as the child grows up. Our friend Marci had such a head start.

Rubbing her eyes, Marci wakes up. It's 1969. She's eleven years old, and all is right in her world. She smiles. As Marci looks around her room, she loves her bright, psychedelic walls with the royal blue shag carpet and chartreuse flowered curtains. Her very tolerant mother let her pick them out herself.

Marci runs into the kitchen and plants a big kiss on her dad's cheek, just as she has every day as long as she can remember. She doesn't think about it, but her life wouldn't feel quite right without this morning ritual, which includes talking with her dad as she eats breakfast. He's never too busy to listen, just as her mother is never too busy to skip tucking her into bed at night. (Asked today to describe her dad, she calls him "the most naturally happy person I've ever known.")

Simple loving gestures help create a warm and safe environment, the most basic need of a small child. Without them, the seed of uncertainty is planted, and in later years it can grow into a sense that you are unsafe and unprotected. Marci feels she can face up to anything. That feeling isn't realistic in an eleven-year-old but it's psychologically very beneficial. Feeling safe and therefore courageous has lasted a lifetime for Marci and led to some remarkable accomplishments.

For eleven-year-old Marci, there seems to be some sort of celebration or holiday observance punctuating every day. She sits with her mom to solve the jumble puzzle in the morning paper before going to school. If she catches a cold and has to stay home, she isn't allowed to mope—there's a board game to play with her mother to keep her spirits up. (Her favorite was Rack-O.)

Over the course of a whole year, the passage of time was marked by birthday parties, weddings, graduations, and anniversaries. Marci's family didn't let these ceremonies casually pass by. People stood up and spoke what they felt in their hearts. The one being honored felt a real validation. There was also religious ritual. The family's faith was Judaism, and she learned the reverence of a high holiday like Yom Kippur and of a cousin's bar mitzvah.

Yom Kippur is the most important holiday in the Jewish calendar. Marci remembers her dad, who demanded very little from others, sitting her down for a serious talk when she was fourteen. She had boldly proclaimed that she had other plans than going to synagogue. She might not even observe Yom Kippur at all anymore.

"You have a lot of freedom," her father told her, "because your mother and I want you to grow up as your own person. Someday you can make any decision you want. But right now you're living with us. Yom Kippur is important in this family, and as long as you're here, we want you to participate."

Marci relented, and because she had a loving bond with her

father, she didn't resent his authority. One stern talk doesn't settle a person's attitude toward religion. As time unfolded, Marci faced the whole issue of Jewishness—and still does—just as Catholics wrestle with the faith of their forebears. On her own she has made the decision to keep observing Yom Kippur, as she still does. For her, the traditional Day of Atonement has become the Day of Oneness. She has given tradition a personal meaning, which is another way that a modern person can relate to time-honored rituals, through a connection to wholeness.

Unlike her father, who was known as the "happy dentist," Marci wasn't born with a naturally sunny disposition. From a young age she remembers feelings of self-doubt and emotional confusion. When she got older and was on her own, she always found herself worrying about finances and uncertainty over the future. Even so, she is quite certain that the foundation rituals in her early life provided her with a sense of security and peace. Without them, her worries might drive her to distraction. But they don't.

"I get anxious like everybody else, perhaps more than most people," she says. "But there's a quiet voice inside me that tells me I'm all right. I never lose that reassurance. It's the greatest gift my family gave me growing up, and yet I know a lot of people who never got such a gift."

The point is this: every life needs a secure foundation, and rituals can play that role. If you didn't gain a strong foundation as a child, you can use ritual as a repair mechanism today. Let's look back at how Marci's story exhibits some key elements. When they are successful, rituals bind people to one another through a shared experience. The stronger the emotions attached to a ritual, the more memorable it will be, sometimes for years to come.

Foundation rituals offer a positive way to fill in the gaps of your childhood experience. If you're typical, your upbringing was wobbly, mixing chaos with order, security with anxiousness, love with pain—a perfect recipe for careless and unconscious living. The remedy is to live with conscious intent today. That's what we are guiding you toward in this book. Hopefully you are beginning to get into your own life rhythm. Congratulations. The road from here only gets more fascinating and fulfilling.

PREPARATION FOR
TRANSFORMATION

To show you how people can be transformed by uncovering their Life Design, we rejoin Marci, the little girl we met in the last chapter. By the time she was thirteen, Marci was clear about one thing: She was going to be a public speaker. She had heard the late Zig Ziglar, a popular motivational speaker, and it was while listening to him that she realized she, too, wanted to spend her life inspiring and uplifting people. After earning an MBA at UCLA, she got a job with a seminar company and for years followed her passion for speaking, traveling from city to city, teaching communication skills in courses at Fortune 500 companies.

Marci's life purpose seemed to fall into her lap, but there were some major hitches.

Looking back, she says, "I began to question everything I was doing. First of all, I was exhausted all the time. I had been pushing myself physically and mentally without respecting what I might be doing to myself. Second, I kept wondering if all this exhausting effort was really worth it. I knew how to teach people better communication skills. But it didn't feel like I was making a real difference in their lives. Wasn't that supposed to be the point?"

As much as she loved being a speaker and trainer, she started getting depressed.

"In my courses I kept meeting people, especially other women, who suffered from low self-esteem, just as I had for so long. I knew everything about how awful it feels to think you're not good enough."

Seeing how deeply she was involved in the problems of her students, Marci could have backed away and continued to protect herself behind the role of teacher and trainer. But instead, she had an "Aha" moment, which led her in the opposite direction.

"If I could learn the secret of how to get over my own low self-esteem, I could pass the knowledge on to others. I would be significantly contributing to their lives. That would be the contribution I'd been missing."

This is the kind of turning point that some people reach but millions don't. Marci stopped being goal-oriented, focusing on the end result. She already had plenty of end results—success, money, a career, and reputation. These had compensated for her low self-esteem but never healed it. Now she saw a different way. She turned her attention to process instead of results. Specifically, she entered the process of discovering who she really was. This was the beginning of uncovering her Life Design.

WHERE YOUR LIFE
DESIGN COMES FROM

We'll pick up Marci's story again in a minute. First, let's look at how Marci began to uncover her Life Design. When anyone has a thrilling "Aha" moment, it seems at first that every question has been answered. But in reality, "Aha" is just the sound a door makes when it swings open. Marci was standing in front of the door, amazed and happy that she had found a new way forward. But what does that mean to you? We believe in modeling our lives on great role

models, yet in the end we all walk our own path. For us, Marci became a kind of role model, especially for the way she confronted her
own low self-esteem. But even more valuable are the new steps she
started to take. They provide an excellent example of the preparation needed to meet your Life Design face-to-face.

Five Steps to Prepare You

Setting the stage for your Life Design:

> *Step 1* Stay connected to what you love.
> *Step 2* Keep track of your energy levels, physical and mental.
> *Step 3* Don't settle for external results.
> *Step 4* Don't identify with your success. Keep asking,
>   "Who am I, really?"
> *Step 5* Honestly and openly face your problems and
>   weaknesses.

You may be surprised that we call these preparatory steps—they
don't exactly look as easy as putting training wheels on a bike. But
the mind has many layers, as does life itself. You can't plunge in
without preparation, just as a deep-sea diver can't throw himself
into the ocean without the right equipment and training. This stage
isn't boring or hard work. "Prepare for your Life Design" is the same
as saying, "Prepare to be amazed." You are infinitely more than you
think you are. It's quite amazing to arrive at the stage where you see
the truth of this.

And you want to know a secret? While these steps are good and
valuable advice, when you regularly and consistently connect with
the transcendental center of your life through meditation or other
activities that allow you to transcend the thinking mind, they de-

velop naturally, without much effort or doing. That's why meditation has been such a gift for us.

Step 1: Stay Connected to What You Love.

This was the core message of our first book, *The Passion Test*. You've probably run across the maxim (it became the title of another popular book) "Do what you love. The money will follow." That's an inspiring philosophy, but it takes a great deal of trust to follow it. Harris polls have found that only 20 percent of American workers felt "passionate" about their work. Gallup found only 29 percent of workers are "engaged" in their work.

What's even more important is the connection you feel to what matters most deeply to you in whatever you are doing. As Nietzsche said, "He who has a why to live for can bear almost any how."

Yet for the vast majority, the need to survive and raise a family drives a belief that money has to come first. Love is put on hold. A recent news story surrounding the economic downturn that began in 2008 reported that more college graduates than ever were choosing to enter the financial and banking fields. Despite the widespread blame directed at Wall Street, students at even the most liberal colleges were headed there (including one out of four Harvard graduates).

Young people are idealistic, typically, so what explains this trend? These graduates have no illusions about Wall Street. They were in it for the money, arguing that after making four or five million in a hurry, they could retire at twenty-five or twenty-six to pursue what they really love. This is a new twist on what older generations have always done: Work until you have a nest egg, then do what you really love after you retire.

We look on the old model, and its new twist, as a recipe for frustration and lack of fulfillment. Connecting to what truly matters to you is the key to fulfilling your Life Design. It's the only way you can stay on track with your unique purpose for being alive. The longer you postpone the people and things you love, the more separated you become from them. More than that, love has its own power and motivation. You will never discover how much this power can do for you unless you test it.

We dream about what we love, and as long as the dream remains a fantasy, it protects us from having to try and fail. It takes something else—love in action—to support and motivate a person. When what you love turns into action, then the dream begins to become a reality. The passion underlying the dream keeps you going through the inevitable failure and frustration that come with making any dream real.

Realizing your dreams requires a process of self-discovery, in which you work through the reasons for not loving yourself until you reach the core where love is unshakable. Then its power can manifest in every area of life.

When you turn love into real action, you set up a feedback loop in your brain, so that the more you do what you love, the more you love what you do. Feedback loops work by input and output, so it's no surprise that the more positive the input, the more positive the output. Besides testing the beliefs of love, you are training your brain to look deeper into love as you evolve.

Step 2: Keep Track of Your Energy Levels, Physical and Mental.

Your Life Design is the source of energy. It has untold reserves of energy, and the more inspired you are, the more energy you tap into. That's why Michelangelo, despite all the discomforts of climbing on scaffolding, lying for hours on his back, and facing a job that would take years to complete, found the energy to paint the Sistine Chapel, while someone assigned to climb the same scaffolding and cover the ceiling in flat white latex paint would soon get bored and tired. Energy can be called physical, but we tap into it subjectively.

You should do work that leaves you feeling energized rather than exhausted. When you are doing work that is aligned with the things that matter most to you, your passions, the meaning in your work gives energy rather than taking it away. Work feels purposeful, and that purpose pulls you onward, allowing you to do things that might seem impossible for others.

We are strong believers in positive energy, and you need to check yourself throughout the day to make sure not simply that you aren't tired, but that your energy hasn't turned negative. The leading indicators are easy to spot once you begin to pay attention to them.

POSITIVE ENERGY

Results in you enjoying what you're doing.

Brings high spirits and enthusiasm.

Bonds you with other people.

Shows your work in a good light, as valuable and worthwhile.

Gives you an optimistic outlook.

Makes you feel vibrant and light.

NEGATIVE ENERGY

Makes you feel bored with what you're doing.

Brings dullness and lack of enthusiasm.

Isolates you from other people.

Shows your work in a bad light as pointless and routine.

Gives you a pessimistic outlook.

Makes you feel tired and weighed down.

As you reveal your Life Design, you'll know firsthand the incredible amount of positive energy that pours out—the secret is that you feel constantly renewed at a deep level, and therefore the energy you need isn't blocked by frustration and inner conflict. It helps in advance to check your energy level in order to face the problems of obstacles and resistance, exhaustion and burnout, depression and mental fatigue. What you want for yourself is a flow of energy that can be sustained and renewed, the same issue that society is facing when allocating its fuel needs. The ingredients that go into your energy needs are mental and physical, so both have to be maximized to produce the best results.

The easiest way to achieve this is what we have called the secret that guarantees a passionate life: "Whenever you're faced with a choice, a decision, or an opportunity, choose in favor of your passions."

Step 3: Don't Settle for External Results.

Results aren't the same as fulfillment. Society mistakenly holds the belief, as promoted in mass media and advertising, that the two are identical. The idea being that the highest salary leads to the greatest happiness, along with the biggest house and the fastest car. But in reality, money only brings you happiness under two conditions, according to psychiatrists. First, you need enough to overcome basic needs of survival and attain a degree of comfort. Second, money leads to happiness only when having the money and the things money can buy is not a burden.

The secret here is to use external results to reach internal aims. Warren Buffett, the most successful investor in America, is famous for living in the same fairly modest house in Omaha where he raised his family. This isn't a deliberate act of self-denial. Buffett simply doesn't use his wealth in a false pursuit of happiness. He sees himself as someone with a special talent for investing, and the satisfaction of letting that talent blossom as it expresses itself is his primary goal. To Buffett, money is a tool for measuring how well he is using his talents, not a goal in itself.

Ernest Hemingway, in describing his work habits during his most successful period in Paris before World War II, when he gained eminence at a very young age, said that he isolated himself in the morning until he had finished half a page. As an external result, half a page would take any average professional writer around fifteen minutes. But Hemingway's standards were incredibly high. To reach them might take three or four hours. The external result was unsatisfactory until it matched his internal purpose.

How is this done in everyday life? We've already mentioned a very important point: If you pursue long-term goals, you'll find greater happiness than from short-term goals. Taking a long time to plan your dream house, for example, will give you satisfaction all along the way, which is different from the brief but intense high you'd get if you were handed the keys to a nice house by a generous wealthy stranger. The external result is the same in both cases, but the internal process is quite different.

Step 3 tells us to find the most satisfying process for reaching external goals. We aren't saying that externals like money and success aren't worthwhile. They figure into our own lives and dreams. Once you uncover your Life Design, you'll be immersed in a process that perfectly balances inner and outer. As preparation, pay attention to this balance as it applies today. External results match inner process when the following indicators appear:

You feel absorbed in what you are doing, lost in your work
   as if it was play.
You love what you do, as reflected in a sense of enthusiasm
   and passion.

Your creative juices are flowing.

The energy surrounding your work is positive.

You feel that your work makes a contribution to the world.

Every step toward the final outcome brings its own
satisfaction.

Step 4: Don't Identify with Your Success—Keep Asking, "Who Am I, Really?"

Success is intoxicating. It makes you feel stronger than not being successful; no one could disagree with that. There are always stories of success gone bad, as we all know from reading about lottery winners, for example, who curse their luck two years later because of changes in their lives that they couldn't handle. It's a myth to say, "I don't have a problem that a million dollars wouldn't solve." Even if you're fortunate enough to maintain some modesty and humility in the wake of your success, the subtler danger centers on what you identify with.

It's fascinating to read studies that find that people driving expensive cars are more likely to ignore crosswalks than those driving inexpensive cars. The drivers break the law because they feel privileged; they can't be bothered by rules that are easy to flout. Other studies took college students and asked them to play a game of Monopoly, with two people to a game, but a change of rules. One player would be given an unfair advantage over the other. He would start out with more money; he'd roll two dice while the other player rolled only one; and he would get higher rewards for passing Go. When put in the privileged position, these players couldn't help but win. The psychological twist is that after a while, people who were given a totally arbitrary advantage began to act as if they deserved it.

This attitude emerged in several ways. They might crow over a good move in the game, taunt other players when they lost money, and act subtly superior. They were also more likely to cheat. Indirectly, there were behavioral changes outside the game. For example, when researchers put a bowl of snacks beside the board, the privileged players took the most from it. They felt entitled to more. We lump all such behavioral changes into a bigger category: identifying with your success.

Identification means "I am X." If you say, "I'm British," you're stating part of your identity. As a simple statement, identifying with your nationality is value free. "I am British" is as neutral as "I am German." But in real life there's very little about nationality that's neutral. Everyone absorbs into their sense of self the ups and downs of their home country. If Great Britain is at war, if its economy takes a dive, if it gets looked upon on the world stage as a bad actor rather than a force for good, then all of these things affect how an English person might feel about himself.

When you base your own identity on such enduring values as love, respect, self-reliance, compassion, service, and so on, your sense of self is more permanent. These values are nourished from within; they are more closely connected to the transcendent center of your Life Design.

Yet society tempts us to identify with external results: how much money you make, what your rank is in the company, where you live, and how big your house is. It's not a temptation you want to give in to, because of the hidden costs.

For example, it's a well-known fact that in relationships, the partner who earns the most money generally feels entitled to say where the money goes. Associated with this is the sociological finding that the toughest issue in troubled marriages is when the woman earns more than the man. In both cases, tension arises from identifying with money, on either the winning or losing side.

The myth persists that hundreds of ruined businessmen jumped out of windows during the Great Depression (the number was low but highly publicized), but what's true is that men are the most likely to define their self-worth by how much they earn. Similarly disturbing is the statistic that after the economic downturn of 2008, suicide rates in the United States increased by as much as 40 percent among white males, which is surmised to be a direct result of rising unemployment.

Step 4 asks us not to say, "I am rich or poor, important or not, successful or not" in terms of external rewards. When you uncover your Life Design, you'll see that your identity isn't bound up with your salary or even your accomplishments. "I" is far more mysterious and changeable. It shifts as you grow and evolve. Ultimately, you will ask "Who am I?" and the answer will be that you are the essence of life. Your awareness is merged with everything, and your life flows like a river, following the course that allows you to fulfill your unique and special purpose. Unlike a river, however, your course isn't fixed; it leads in unexpected directions, making every day fresh and new.

As preparation, you can see yourself in terms of the constant change that is actually you. Here are some statements that may help you stay grounded in the larger reality of who you are:

Who I Am, Right This Minute

I am a different person than I was yesterday.
I am a process that is always unfolding.
I am a story that has new chapters to reveal.
I am part of the flow of life.
I am one thread in the tapestry of the universe.
I am the unknown, constantly seeing itself in new ways.
I am the game of life and the play of creation.

Step 5: Honestly Face Your Problems and Weaknesses.
To be blunt, feeling good about yourself is easy—you just have to ignore everything that isn't so good. This is the course of least resistance, but it takes a toll. All the negative feelings you shove down out of sight will return one day. Trying to pretend that you have no problems only makes them worse. The way to feel good about yourself that actually works is to take an honest look at parts of your life that bring you unhappiness so that you can work on them.

"Work" implies effort and struggle, which is why most people don't resolve their issues—they assume it's too hard. Yet in another light, what is more fascinating than proving to yourself that you can grow stronger and become the person you really want to be?

Assume, because it's true, that you were designed to grow and evolve. There's no doubt that this was true as you grew from childhood. The only difference when it comes to being an adult is that your parents aren't there to protect you when you fall. More important, a child can't help but develop physically—nobody has a choice not to experience the throes of puberty, for example. (We like the joke that goes, "I refuse to believe in reincarnation if it means going through junior high again.")

As an adult, you have the choice to grow or not, and if you do choose to grow, your development will be mental, emotional, and spiritual, not physical. Now that neuroscience has revealed that thoughts and emotions alter the brain, the strict division between mental and physical no longer exists. Even so, your Life Design, the perfect model for future growth, reveals itself in the mind by giving you new thoughts, feelings, hopes, wishes, and insights.

To take advantage of your Life Design, you must be comfortable with looking at your inner world. If it's a place you avoid, fearing what you will find if you look at yourself too closely, that's understandable. But the secret of your Life Design is that it isn't scary or negative in any way. The power it contains is totally for your good, which means that only your personal growth, and not tearing yourself down, is at issue. It takes conscious intent to say, "I will remain aware every day of how I really feel," but once you begin, the experience will bring you more and more into alignment with your own true essence and in that, your life's purpose.

The problems and weaknesses that all of us face can be put into a few basic categories:

Things we're afraid of.
Things we're angry about.
Things that confuse us.
Things we believe we can't change.

From these categories spring anxiety, self-doubt, frustration, and victimization. We aren't asking you to solve these issues, only to be aware of them. It would be totally unreasonable to tell you that you must be problem-free before you can uncover your Life Design. The whole point is exactly the reverse; if you're aware of a problem, your Life Design will bring a solution. The key is awareness. What you aren't aware of, you can't change.

In terms of practicality, here's a simple ritual you can follow every day. Whenever you feel upset, stop for a moment and ask yourself the following:

"Am I upset because I'm feeling anxious and afraid?"
"Am I upset because I'm feeling anger and resentment?"
"Am I upset because I'm confused about something?"
"Am I upset because I've hit a wall and can't change the situation?"

These questions bring you back to yourself in a realistic way. The next step is to sit quietly and actually be with whatever you're feeling. Don't try to repress it; at the same time, don't lash out at anyone else. As you sit, watch your feelings and be present in your body. Do this quiet awareness exercise for five minutes.

Finally, if you still find that you're upset, take the following mental actions.

Fear If you're feeling anxious in a given situation, breathe deeply. Once you feel calmer, ask yourself if your fear is reasonable or simply personal. If it's reasonable, then start taking steps to get rid of the reason. If your rent is due and you can't pay it, for example, which would make most people anxious, call your landlord, ask for an extension, and then seek a loan from someone. On the other hand, if your fear is personal, pledge to work on it as an issue that needs to be addressed. There is no need to live with fear, reasonable or personal. Getting rid of your fears is a big project for anyone, but the best start is to bring awareness to the problem, because awareness is more powerful than you imagine.

Anger If you're angry in a certain situation, first sit and be with your feeling for five minutes, as above. Make sure you're alone. Don't listen to the voice in your head that shouts, "I'm right to be angry." Thoughts always justify feelings. As long as you're feeling angry, your thoughts will tell you that you're right. But right and wrong aren't the issue. Anger is destructive to the happiness of both yourself and the person you want to blame. Getting the destructive energy out of the way is what you're aiming for.

After your anger has calmed somewhat—take as much time as you need for this to happen—assess it. Is anger a reasonable response in the situation? If it is, then look for a solution after you've calmed down. Let's say that someone junior to you at work has been promoted above you. Responding with anger could be reasonable, but you won't find out why the promotion happened by storming into your boss's office. Only when you have gotten past your anger can you explore what's going on and why.

The world contains a lot of angry people who need very little to set them off. If you're one of these people, it will help to see that your anger is personal. It's yours to deal with, not the world's, because there will always be wrong and injustice in the world. When you recognize that you use anger as a weapon, excuse, tactic for domination, or purely for the pleasure of venting, becoming aware that your anger is ultimately destructive, both for you and for others, will help you change harmful patterns.

Confusion People are confused—or say they are—for many different reasons. We've all met someone who backs out of confrontations with, "I'm confused. I see reasons for both sides to think they're right." This isn't so much confusion as not wanting to get involved. Then there are people who use the line "I'm trying to understand you, but you're confusing me." This is usually a tactic to make the other person feel wrong without coming straight out and saying so.

But there is genuine confusion, too, and we've all been thrown into it. If you see your spouse having lunch with a stranger, and both are laughing over a glass of wine, you have a right to be confused until an explanation is offered. On a larger stage, the world's problems are so complex that the only reasonable way to react is by being confused. (There's a parody of Kipling's uplifting poem "If" that begins, "If you can keep your head when all about you are losing theirs . . . you probably don't understand the situation.")

Personal confusion is the sort you need to address. It takes some familiar forms:

Self-doubt. You don't feel competent enough, smart enough, or good enough.

Insecurity. You aren't sure that you are safe and protected.

Low self-esteem. You aren't sure you matter.

Suspicion, skepticism. You aren't sure that the truth is as it seems.

Lack of trust. You aren't sure you can really rely on anybody.

Lack of direction. You aren't sure what path to take that will bring more fulfillment.

The emergence of your Life Design brings with it an abiding sense of security and safety that allows you to release your confusion and doubt. You will discover that what you've been suffering from is confusion about the nature of life and your role in it. As you gain clarity about the nature of life, doubt disappears and a sense that life is supporting you grows.

Things you can't change. In the realm of problems and weaknesses, the most destructive force is fear, but the second most destructive is frustration. When you feel helpless to change something, frustration mounts, and if it continues, you find yourself becoming resigned, resentful, passive, blocked, angry, and depressed.

For some people the whole sequence is so familiar that they've given up on creating any kind of meaningful change. "This is just me. I can't do anything about it." But change isn't really the issue. You're already a bundle of change. New thoughts and feelings constantly stream into your head. Millions of chemical messages are being sent from your brain to every cell in your body.

The real issue is directed change, using conscious intent to get what you want out of life. If handling change has been a challenge for you, initiate the following ritual: Stop for a moment whenever you have the feeling that nothing is changing or ever will. Say to yourself, "I am always changing. I can choose how I change. My greatest ally is my awareness, and as it expands, what I really want will come to me of its own accord." Then ask yourself, "What evidence can I find in my life that this is true?" See if you can find at least three pieces of evidence, first, that life is always changing, and, second, that as your awareness expands, what you really want begins to come of its own accord.

Your mind is constantly seeking to find evidence to support your embedded beliefs. By consciously choosing to change your beliefs and then finding evidence to support the new belief, you will begin to shift the way you experience life.

MARCI'S TRANSFORMATION

Now that you know how to prepare for transformation, what's it like to actually be transformed? To give an example, we'll pick up Marci's story again. She was on the verge of discovering her Life Design, although she didn't know in advance that such a drastic change was about to occur.

One thing Marci did know: her life was in flux. She had made the decision to face one of her main weaknesses, low self-esteem. Being a person of action, she scoured the country until she discovered a then little-known trainer named Jack Canfield. Jack's Self Esteem Seminars were among the most respected on the subject. This was 1989, four years before Jack co-authored a little book called *Chicken Soup for the Soul*.

Marci took Jack's courses, adopted him as her mentor, and was soon traveling the country, giving self-esteem workshops. She felt good that she was making a greater contribution to people's lives than before, and her own self-esteem issues were starting to be healed. She was definitely more aligned with what she loved doing.

But as she looks back, Marci saw that she was caught in a familiar trap. "After years of teaching self-esteem programs, my life was still one of nonstop travel, living out of a suitcase, and staring at the four walls of hotel rooms. Back-to-back seminars were killing me."

One of her best friends, Jani, intervened, telling her, "You can't keep going like this, Marci. You're looking exhausted and burned out. That's not good for a transformational speaker."

Marci knew that Jani was right, and even though it ran against the grain for her to slow down, she accepted her friend's invitation to go to a seven-day silent meditation retreat in the mountains. She confessed to herself that in her drive to help other people and motivate them to change, she had forgotten to take care of herself, and the changes she saw in herself weren't necessarily all positive. But something deeper was at work. A voice in her head repeated the same question again and again: "Is this all there is?"

She says, "I've always been able to find the next step that moved my career ahead. Deep inside I knew my friend was right. But what I actually said was, 'Jani, are you insane?' Seven days of silence? I wasn't even sure I'd last."

Speakers are born to speak. A week of pure, unadulterated torture lay ahead. And yet Marci knew she was at the end of her rope.

Jani tried to reassure her. "I know this is scary, but if you want something new to come into your life, you have to change your approach. As exhausted as you are right now, if the perfect idea bit you on the nose, you wouldn't know it." (We're not sure she actually said "nose.") So Marci told herself that she was going for a rest cure, or rather the modern version, electronic renunciation: no television, no computers, no phones, no anything.

The week of silence that she dreaded turned out to be the biggest breakthrough of her life. We'll present all the details in the next chapter. What we'd like to point out is something applicable to you, as different as your story may be from hers.

Invisible forces were organizing events to bring Marci to the perfect place where she needed to be in her life. This isn't a mystical belief. Hidden from us are the deeper layers of the mind. We pass our days thinking, feeling, and saying things from a superficial level of the mind, because everyday affairs mostly don't demand anything else. Routines feel empty when things like the following happen:

You spend your time in mindless, automatic tasks.
You repeat the same thoughts, words, and actions.
You don't feel fulfilled.
You aren't growing.

Despite her success in her chosen career, Marci was haunted by these lacks in her life. Discontent can be a powerful trigger. It was, in her case, and without writing down a plan, Marci unconsciously prepared herself for what was coming next, her big breakthrough. She followed the things we've suggested to you. She remained aware of her problems and weaknesses. She honestly confronted her real feelings. She didn't identify with her outward success. She was willing to look beyond externals to ask, "Who am I? Why am I here?"

In response, a deeper part of herself was about to wake up. She had prepared the way for transformation, and now transformation was here.

YOUR "AHA" MOMENT, AND HOW TO GET THERE

W hen we last left Marci, she had begun a weeklong medita-tion retreat that required complete silence. Once she arrived at the meditation center, which was in a quiet woodland setting in the Catskills, Marci wasn't happy. During the first four days of the re-treat, her biggest fears about going into silence were realized.

She says, "Everything about it was excruciating. Writing notes helped some—it was the only way we were allowed to communicate with each other. But my friend Jani, who coaxed me there in the first place, wouldn't write back, nor would anyone else. I was like a lioness trapped in a cage, counting the days until I could talk again."

The only thing that made it bearable was settling into a daily routine that felt extremely healthy and relaxing. This routine closely resembled what we described in our program of foundation rituals: going to bed early, rising with the sun, doing yoga exercises, and meditating. Light vegetarian food was served at meals, followed by a walk in the woods afterward.

Marci laughs as she recalls, "It was like a spa with a gag order."

The silence was maddening. Whenever she thought she couldn't keep at it anymore, she just remembered her initial instruction the day she arrived: "Stay with the routine." She did, and to Marci's surprise, her discomfort began to lift. Little by little, she felt layers of fatigue fall away. Her old energy, excitement, and enthusiasm for life began to return.

"I was quite relieved. A nagging fear in the back of my mind was that I had become a permanent burnout case. Of course, all this newfound energy made me want to run away from there as fast as I could."

She reminded herself that her sense of renewal had come from the routine she was following, and so she kept going. Then, on day four, in the middle of her meditation, a lightbulb went off in her head. Inspiration had struck. She had an idea that she knew, instantly and with total certainty, would be worth a million dollars or more. But because of the promise she'd made to Jani to observe silence for all seven days, there wasn't a darned thing she could do but wait it out before she could tell anyone or act on it. Finally, on the morning of the eighth day, when the course was over, Marci sprinted past Jani like a roadrunner on steroids and pounced on the nearest pay phone.

The person she was dialing was Jack Canfield, co-author of *Chicken Soup for the Soul*, which had become a mega-bestseller. She had made a connection with him after attending his seminars on self-esteem, and in the intervening years Canfield had become her mentor.

The moment he answered the phone, she blurted out, "Jack! I've got it. *Chicken Soup for the Woman's Soul.*"

She held her breath, waiting for him to reply, and what he said sent a huge wave of relief over her. "What a great idea! I can't believe no one has thought of it before."

In that moment the most popular nonfiction book series of all time was born.

FINDING YOUR OWN
BREAKTHROUGH

What would inspire a breakthrough in your life? It's a tricky question, since every person is unique. For centuries inspiration was thought to come from a higher power—God or the gods, the muses, or angels—and we struggle today to find an explanation that works for modern, rational people. The answer lies in your unique Life Design. If you recall, one circle in the Life Design is about knowingness, or intuition. Everyone has moments when they just know, without any rational thought, that something is right. It could be love at first sight or a premonition about a future event. All the tumblers click, and suddenly the lock falls open. What the Life Design tells us is that these "Aha" moments are not accidental. They represent a specific potential—knowingness—built into the mind itself.

Marci found her breakthrough in a flash of inspiration that came out of the blue—in her excitement, that's how it felt. But, in fact, her "Aha" moment was carefully prepared for in advance. Let's recap what actually happened.

Relaxation: Marci relinquished her hectic life and took time out to let mind and body relax.

Reconnection: She had no external outlets except her daily routine and walks in the woods. This gave Marci an opportunity to reconnect with herself.

Flow: The regularity of the routine put her back into the natural flow of her biorhythms and the cycle of sunrise and sunset, which have a powerful effect on the physiology.

Silence: She was thrown back onto herself, which was panic inducing at first. But after a time Marci realized that silence is a natural state of the mind at rest.

Meditation: She set time aside to dive deeper into silence, the source of creativity and insight.

These are the building blocks of "Aha" moments as outlined by spiritual masters in ancient traditions around the world for thousands of years. The end result for Marci Shimoff was that she became the woman's face for *Chicken Soup for the Soul*—her books in the series and the ones she's subsequently written on her own have spent 118 weeks on the *New York Times* best-seller list and sold fifteen million copies worldwide—but to reach this end point, everything was about process. Now Marci takes time each year to go into silence.

"I'm efficient about it," she says with a smile. "If four days worked before, that should be enough now. It's still a challenge to do a whole week."

Marci has also personalized the foundation rituals that work for her, and she's religious about observing them, no matter how much running around the day might bring. Every morning she begins by making her "green drink"—a multi-ingredient concoction whizzed up in a blender from fresh spinach, kale, celery, blanched almonds, avocado, cucumber, coconut milk, and a little stevia for sweetener. Marci's morning rituals also include an oil massage, meditation, a prayer, a short devotional ceremony, and, at least three or four times a week, her very favorite form of exercise, Zumba.

We've tasted the green drink and, believe it or not, she's won us over. It's delicious. Her foundation rituals are a model of the very things that brought Marci her big breakthrough. If we translate these into our life, here's what you need to do:

Relax: This means a complete stop in your activity, sitting alone, and letting go of the day's stress and fatigue. Don't wait until the end of the day for this. Ideally, you should relax the moment you notice any dullness and lack of energy. Few of us think we can afford that, but we can take five to ten minutes three times a day to enjoy peace and quiet.

Reconnect: It's easy to forget that we are all children of nature, and that our bodies are tied to the cycles of the sun, moon, tides, seasons, and more. (Medical researchers have even discovered a new kind of cell in the retina that is keyed especially to the sky's shade of blue; it evolved so that your body's internal clock can remain attuned to sunrise and sunset.) Even a few minutes a day spent outdoors, maybe lying on the grass and gazing at the sky, serves to reconnect you to your source.

Get into the flow: Nature flows effortlessly, as reflected in the easy way that your cells orchestrate thousands of chemical reactions every second. The brain operates just as effortlessly, but we assume we have to intervene. Every time you doubt, criticize, argue, resist, and throw up obstacles, your ego has become part of a struggle that doesn't need to exist. So it's valuable to do what you can to catch yourself before you jump into the fray, back away, and remind yourself that life is a flow, and the best way to live is in the flow.

Find your silence: Going to a weeklong retreat isn't easily available to everyone, but that's not the only place where silence is found. The real silence is inside you. It gets buried by layers of mental activity, and as long as you keep feeding this activity, your silence will be buried even deeper. On the other hand, outer silence helps uncover inner silence. To put this into practice, find time every day to soak up the complete silence of a church or chapel, a noiseless room, or even your basement. Sit with your eyes closed for ten minutes, simply enjoying the silence—let it refresh you and don't mind the inevitable thoughts that come and go.

Meditate: There are many ways to meditate, and not all are equal. Our preferred method is TM, or the Transcendental Meditation® technique, for many reasons. It is non-religious and has no overtones of practices lifted from another culture. (We personally love India, but that shouldn't be a requirement for learning to meditate.) TM is a modernized version of the most profound meditation practices in India, going back thousands of years. It has the beauty of being simple and practical for relaxing the mind.

But at the same time you tap into the complex matrix of your Life Design, because as the name implies, you enter the transcendent region at the very heart of the mandala. As you keep meditating, TM practice proves to you that this transcendent region is the very source of creativity and intelligence. And if you need external validation, the hundreds of scientific studies published in peer-reviewed journals validate its benefits. Thus, for us, TM has been invaluable for opening up every aspect of our lives.

Because it requires hands-on teaching from a qualified instructor, we can't show you how to practice the TM technique here. Every city and most sizable towns have TM teachers and usually a center where you can go for instruction. You can get connected with a teacher near you by going to www.tm.org. We strongly recommend that you go this route.

RITUAL PRACTICE

Alternate Nostril Breathing

As an interim practice, you can benefit from a simple ritual that is immediately calming. Close your eyes, sit quietly, and perform the gentle exercise known as "alternate nostril breathing" (see diagrams):

Using your right hand, lightly place the thumb against your

right nostril and your last two fingers against your left nostril (the two middle fingers will be folded toward your palm).

You are going to breathe in and out normally, but as you do, you will inhale through one nostril and exhale through the other. It's quite simple once you get the knack. First, press lightly against your left nostril and inhale through the right. Next, press the right nostril closed and exhale through the left nostril. Without changing your finger position, inhale through the left nostril, then press it closed so that you can exhale through the right. Repeat, breathing easily, for five to ten minutes. After that time

you can also sit with your eyes still closed and appreciate your inner quietness. Come out of your meditative state gradually, taking a few deep breaths and opening your eyes slowly. It's also helpful not to rush immediately into vigorous activity.

This breathing ritual comes from India, where it is known as *suryanadisuddhi pranayama*. There are many variations, but the one given here does a very nice job settling the mind, because our breathing is so intimately connected to bringing the brain to a settled state. The key is to let the calming effect arise naturally. If you feel short of breath or want to gulp some air through your mouth, that's perfectly okay. Don't rush, don't push yourself. Your goal is to allow your mind to settle down on its own, effortlessly.

Also, don't mind if you fall asleep before the time is up. Most people have so much hidden fatigue that wants to escape that it grabs the first opportunity. Sleep in this case is beneficial as a way of releasing stress.

Marci's story continued to unfold her Life Design. Material success doesn't mean that she reached the end of the journey, not by any means. The real fruits of her breakthrough began to appear in other areas. For example, her life was filled with amazing serendipitous events. Strangers on a plane would be exactly the people she needed to connect with. She would be having a problem, and into her lap would fall the answer. She'd be the first to tell you that she believes her rituals connect her with her spiritual center daily, and that this connection is the source of all the many blessings she enjoys.

In our language, we would say that Marci's rituals keep her aligned and connected with her unique Life Design. Her alignment results in the confluence of events that create unlikely but always beneficial outcomes. For example, once a year Marci calls on Master Yau, a Chinese master of feng shui, to help make sure that her home is arranged to support her success, prosperity, and happiness. Even so, she was surprised when a major breakthrough happened in her business after she made what seemed like a minor change in her surroundings.

Marci had moved into a new house a year earlier, and Master Yau came for his annual visit. He frowned and said in a frustrated tone, "You haven't moved the large mirror in your office as I told you to last year."

"I love that mirror," Marci pleaded. "It makes the room seem larger, and it reflects the beautiful view of the San Francisco Bay."

But when Master Yau wouldn't budge, she asked the gardeners who happened to be working at her house to help her move the huge mirror into the living room, where he had said it would be okay. When Master Yau initially told her to remove the mirror from her office, Marci was trying to get a contract for a PBS show. The project was stuck, running into one delay after another. Finally, she gave up in frustration, and she hadn't heard from PBS in nine months.

An hour after moving the mirror, the phone rang. It was the people from PBS calling out of the blue. "We just had a meeting, and we've decided to fully fund your show." She was floored.

Was moving a mirror the reason Marci's show came through? Here's what she has to say: "I know in my heart that it's by bringing the sacred into my life through rituals that so many amazing things have happened. It's provided a safe haven for me, a sense of dependability, and a connection to my family and friends that is absolutely precious."

We've already presented a lot to encourage you to align yourself with your Life Design, too. The proof of the pudding is in the eating, they say. So we accept the challenge of giving you a breakthrough that creates your own "Aha" moment. When such a moment occurs, change is no longer a struggle or a distant dream that never comes true. Change will feel natural and effortless, and, in some indefinable way, "right."

THE OBSTRUCTED LIFE DESIGN

Alignment with your Life Design doesn't mean you won't have any challenges. The ups and downs of life are part of what makes walking the path so interesting. The difference is that when you're aligned with your Life Design, obstacles throw you off only briefly, because you have such a strong sense of purpose. Challenges become opportunities rather than insurmountable barriers.

You saw before (refer back to page 16) that the Life Design

diagram has a center point with five circles surrounding it, representing the five levels through which your spiritual core expresses itself: bliss, knowingness, mind, energy, and material form. The center point is your core of pure consciousness, where all possibilities exist. Life energy flows outward from the center as your faint thoughts, wishes, and dreams turn into conscious intentions. A child playing with a toy fire truck who grows up to be a fireman; another child who feels so loved that she wants to be the perfect mother one day; the boy who has a blind cousin and resolves to become a doctor—these intentions are born deep inside and then find their way out into the world. Every accomplishment requires steps that are physical, mental, emotional, and, yes, spiritual (defining spiritual as whatever you are most devoted to and truly revere).

Unfortunately, these "four gates" can be blocked, which is the cause of problems. Blockages are the result of bottled-up emotions, negative conditioning, overwhelming stress, or other obstacles somewhere in the Life Design. When we say, for example, that someone is blind with rage, a blockage is at work. The level of the mind can't be accessed because everything is temporarily bottled up at the emotional level. That's when a person's Life Design becomes distorted and extremely uncomfortable. Imagine a young man drifting aimlessly without a job, feeling like an outcast with no opportunities in sight. His situation could be represented like the diagram on the opposite page.

The coherence of the Life Design is lost. The bulging lines represent how inner distortion may spill out into a person's outer life in society. There is no coherence between the person's inner and outer existence. This is the kind of disconnect that makes people feel hollow and inauthentic. As a result, what's happening inside feels so uncomfortable that it may pop out into the world as anger, aggression, or other destructive behaviors. The four gates of the physical, mental, emotional, and spiritual life are so blocked that access to their center isn't open.

But the thing to notice is that no matter what has happened in one's life until now, the core of your Life Design remains untouched. In the diagram below, the four gates are blocked, creating distortion in this person's inner and outer life, but the transcendent core and five rings that surround it are undisturbed. All that is required is to unblock the four gates, and then the power, intelligence, and creativity of the transcendent will once again flow through one's life.

We've offered an extreme example, but for most people there is enough blockage that damage is done, all stemming from their inability to find the core self—often they don't even accept that such a thing as the transcendent even exists. Needless to say, many people do not experience the bliss that emanates from the center—only

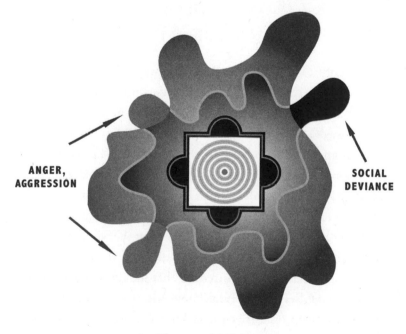

An Obstructed Life Design

unhappiness and frustration, along with a vague urge to keep seeking and searching. But if they don't know what direction to take, seeking turns empty. The only reliable guide, the Life Design, isn't available. All the components of the self are still there, however. They can't be permanently stifled. No matter what may have happened in one's life, no matter how distressed a person's life may have become, the inner structure of one's Life Design remains intact and can be accessed. It's just a matter of removing the blocks that have obstructed the four gates.

These blocks create a state of confusion in which the mind sends mixed messages. Let's look more closely at these, because clarity is the basis for going forward. "When you are clear, what you want will show up in your life, and only to the extent that you are clear" (from *The Passion Test*).

CORE BELIEFS

Perfect clarity can dawn in a flash, the way it does in *A Christmas Carol* when the loveless Scrooge wakes up to how terribly he has wasted his life. Such "Aha" moments give hope, because they point the way to reconnecting with one's Life Design. Why do some people get an "Aha" moment that changes their lives, while others don't? A lot has to do with beliefs and attitudes. What if you believe in the cliché that life is unfair? Such a belief is pessimistic and turns you into a victim waiting for the next bad thing to happen. There's the old joke every medical student hears about the woman who goes to her doctor, afraid that she has cancer. After a thorough physical and a barrage of tests, he reassures her that she doesn't have cancer. Six months later the woman is back, once again certain that she has cancer. Once again tests are run, and her doctor tells her that she's perfectly fine.

This goes on for years, until the woman is past sixty. She goes to her doctor with her usual fears, only this time he has bad news for her. Her tests show signs of cancer. To which she replies, "See? I told you!"

The moral of the story is that anticipating the worst is a terrible waste of life. The present slips through your fingers when you worry about the future. Beliefs that are life supporting move you forward; they make today better. Be willing to accept that you live in a friendly universe, and that life is organized to support you. Doesn't it make sense that life in such a universe should have the potential to be fun and easy?

We all know people who are sure that the world is falling apart. They constantly look for proof that their pessimism is justified. What do they find? Every day more proof of how horrible life actually is. This constant reinforcement creates what is known as *core beliefs*.

A core belief is more than a deep conviction. It contains something *that must be so*. Many people throughout recorded history have held the belief that they are separate individuals, apart from the people and world around them. This core belief guided their actions. It was the basis for jealousy, for envy, for war, for greed, and a host of other issues. Some people transcended this core belief through their belief in an omnipresent God. Through that core belief they saw themselves and their world as interconnected. Today, as modern physics delves into the most basic nature of life, even science suggests that separation is an artifact of sensory experience, not reality. And so more and more people are adopting the belief that life is an interconnected whole. Core beliefs can be positive or negative. Their common feature is that they unconsciously guide our thoughts and actions.

If we ask ourselves why more people aren't having "Aha" moments, the biggest reason is that their core beliefs are blocking the way. Let's make this personal. Look at the list of core beliefs below. It contains both positive and negative core beliefs. Which ones do you hold, not just casually but deep down in your heart? Be honest with yourself, since that's the first step in changing your core beliefs.

What Are Your Core Beliefs?

From the following list, check off any core belief, positive or negative, that you would call one of your own.

- [ ] 1. I am unique, unlike anyone else in the world.
- [ ] 2. After I die, that's the end.
- [ ] 3. I have something special to offer.
- [ ] 4. What happens is mostly random. It's pointless to look for a hidden meaning.
- [ ] 5. I am here to grow and evolve.
- [ ] 6. Life is just what you see. There's no higher plan.
- [ ] 7. I deserve the great things I want for myself.
- [ ] 8. Human nature always contains some evil or darkness.
- [ ] 9. I am lovable.
- [ ] 10. I'm scared to get too close to someone else. It's safer to keep my distance.
- [ ] 11. Intimacy is a wonderful thing. I want more.
- [ ] 12. I'll consider myself lucky if somebody loves me and wants to have me.
- [ ] 13. There is a spark of goodness in everyone.
- [ ] 14. I don't expect great things for myself. They're just a dream.
- [ ] 15. I am playing my part in a larger plan, even if I can't always see what the big picture is.
- [ ] 16. People never really change.

☐ 17. Life has a purpose; it's not meaningless.
☐ 18. I don't have anything special to offer.
☐ 19. After I die, I will go to a better place. Death isn't the end.
☐ 20. I'm ordinary. My life is nothing special.

SCORING:
Count the number of checks you made in the odd-numbered items (1, 3, 5, etc.). These are your positive core beliefs. Total _____

Count the number of checks you made in the even-numbered items (2, 4, 6, etc.). These are your negative core beliefs. Total _____

There's no good or bad score to this quiz, but it will tell you several things, beginning with how much your positive outlook is counterbalanced by negative beliefs. We're all complicated creatures, so no one is completely positive or negative. Sometimes we even hold contradictory beliefs on the same issues.

But positive, negative, or undecided, your core beliefs shape how you see the world—and yourself—to the core of your being. We firmly believe that this is not a final judgment. As your Life Design emerges, your core beliefs will shift and become more positive, because negative beliefs are the result of a distorted flow of life energy. Remove the distortions, and the whole picture is transformed.

Once you've checked off the things you believe in, save the list. After you've read this book and absorbed the content, look back at your beliefs one at a time. Ask yourself,

Does this belief *have* to be true?
What makes this belief so convincing?
Do I want to hold a more useful belief?

By asking these questions, you are starting to be conscious of your underlying motives and drives. Core beliefs are unconscious, which is why they are so powerful. Let's take a belief from the negative column: *I'll consider myself lucky if somebody loves me and wants to have me.* For many people, this is a deep-seated belief. Some people will even endure an abusive relationship because, unconsciously, they believe they are so unlovable that they deserve such treatment.

Less extreme but still damaging is the obsession with body image. Girls grow up seeing images of the perfect supermodel body, and when they can't attain this ideal, they lose self-esteem. It's a small step from "I don't like my body" to "I'm not lovable." All kinds of problems, from eating disorders to sexual promiscuity and depression, can follow. Beliefs are triggers. They aren't passive. A single core belief can trigger all kinds of behaviors that you don't even recognize as being linked to it. Think back to Marci at the start of her journey, when she became a successful speaker teaching people in business how to communicate. On the surface, success is success. There was nothing to examine beneath the surface, until she noticed how driven and exhausted she was.

Being driven to the point where you don't take care of yourself usually means that you're running away from something. When Marci looked at herself, she realized what she was running away from was low self-esteem. Where does low self-esteem come from? A huge factor is the core belief "I am not lovable." A negative core belief is like a wall you can't climb over or knock down. It simply blocks your way. For a person who believes "I am unlovable," the block is tragic, because they will spend months and years pursuing behaviors that lead to everywhere but love. Here's a story to illustrate how that works.

Lori played the part of a winner even though deep down she was sure she was a loser. This core belief was deeply rooted going back to her childhood.

"I grew up in a big Catholic family," Lori says. "My mother was the rock that held the family together, just as my grandmother had been for her, growing up. My father was a machinist, and he had issues with having a hot temper and drinking too much. But my mother loved him to pieces, the way she loved all four kids.

"My role as the oldest girl was to be a kind of second mother. By the time I was eight I knew how to change the baby's diapers and load the washing machine. When the other kids were out playing, I ran home from school as quick as I could, just in case my mother needed me. That was my role; I didn't know any other way."

Lori looks back and sees that she grew up too fast. Her mother confided in her about her husband's drinking. She made no effort to keep adult problems separate. In addition, Lori had a congenital hip defect that gave her a slight limp.

"I saw in my mother's eyes how bad she felt about my limp, as if she'd caused it by something she did while pregnant. Her doctor told her it wasn't her fault, but she became protective of me. She was keeping me home because I wasn't exactly like the other girls at school."

Anyone can sympathize with how Lori grew up; her mother was doing the best she could to hold the family together. But as time passed, a core belief began to build up inside Lori: *I'm not good enough.* As it sank in, year by year, this core belief found plenty of reasons to justify itself. What made her not good enough? She wasn't as pretty as the prettiest girl at school. Her father didn't earn much money. His temper and his drinking sometimes led to embarrassing scenes out in public. Her mother wasn't very happy, yet no matter how hard Lori tried to be the best helper in the world, she couldn't change that. The limp was only one ingredient in a picture that became more and more convincing.

By the time she left home at eighteen to go to a state college, Lori was quite confused about herself. She marked this down to typical adolescent doubts, but it became clear that it wasn't that.

"I went off to college thinking I could handle anything, thanks to feeling that I was already an adult by the time I was eleven. I called home all the time, and I kept reassuring my mother that I was fine. But in fact the change was hard for me. I was in a new situation where the course work was a lot harder than in high school, the other girls were entering into serious sexual relationships, and nobody was really my friend. I became more withdrawn, and my grades started to sink. Pretty soon I was feeling miserable, with no one to turn to."

Lori's phone calls home became fewer and fewer. She started keeping to herself and missing class. The downward spiral happened very fast. She refused to come home for Christmas, which alarmed her parents.

"I was too ashamed. I didn't want them to see what a mess I was. I lied and said that I had met a girl who wanted me to come home with her for Christmas, and that her family was very rich. But actually I spent Christmas curled up all day under my desk with the curtains drawn."

A dorm proctor found Lori and recognized how much trouble she was in. Her parents were notified, and Lori went home with them, officially taking the semester off.

"But I never went back," she says. "For two months I could barely drag myself out of bed. My parents were very worried, and they had no clue why I had fallen apart. I didn't, either."

She went to a clinic that offered free sessions with a psychological therapist. They started to talk, and at one point the therapist asked a question that set off a lightbulb in Lori's head.

"She asked me if I had a boyfriend. I said no. Then she asked why not. I stared at her, not knowing what to say. We were both silent for a couple of minutes, then in a softer voice, she asked, 'Don't you think you're lovable?' All I could do was burst out crying."

Lori had the courage and honesty to take a hard look at herself. "I was storing a lot of shame. All those years I had tried so hard to be the best little girl in the world, but in my heart of hearts I had absorbed this fixation that I was damaged goods."

Lori hadn't reached "Aha" yet, but her whole focus was now on changing "I'm not good enough" to "I really am good enough." She promoted this change through daily rituals with the conscious intent of healing herself.

First, she kept a journal of all the good things that happened to her.

Second, she confronted her isolation by going out and doing the things she really loved, one of which was cooking. (She got a job in a local restaurant as a prep chef.)

Third, she made time for self-care. If she had moments when she felt bad about herself, she called a friend she had met in therapy, someone she really trusted. She and her friend would talk about how she felt until Lori was able to part the dark clouds hanging over her.

As she was promoting change in these ways, she found a woman chef at the restaurant who embodied strength and self-reliance along with real self-esteem. She asked this woman to be her mentor, and she agreed. As she felt stronger, she also began to go out to meet men socially. To make sure that the setting wasn't fraught with sexual overtones, the way a singles bar is, Lori chose a church group that did volunteer work.

Healing rituals are part of a rich tradition in every ancient culture. Their loss in modern times is more than regrettable. We have lost a powerful connection between mind and body. Lori had to invent her own rituals from scratch, and she was fortunate to create good ones. She had enough consciousness about her situation to organize her intention with purpose and discipline. Given the chaos that filled her mind when she fell apart at school, it's a testimony to the mind's craving for peace that her instincts served her so well.

One of the themes running through all these rituals was her decision to follow what she loved. "When I first opened up to my therapist, it was shattering," she says. "It would have been so easy to go home and say, 'I'm a head case now. I have all these problems. Maybe it's hopeless.'" This was a trap, as Lori intuitively saw. "I could be a case forever, always working on my problems." Instead, she took steps to affirm who she was. Her decision to do what she really loved was a huge part of her recovery.

Lori wasn't fortunate like Marci, whose family provided a healthy foundation. Lori was so busy growing up too soon that she never experienced the rites of passage that help children feel safe and secure. She had to help run the household even when it was her birthday, and holidays were always tinged with the possibility that her father's behavior might get out of control. Even these basic rituals that are part of most people's lives were torn from her.

If we step back and look at Lori's negative beliefs, what stands out is how one core belief trumped them all: *Life is bad, and that's just how it is.* When you strip anyone's beliefs down to the nub, they are generally about "life is bad" versus "life is good." These are absolute statements that paint a picture in black and white. As rational adults, we all learn that things are relative, painted in shades of gray. But core beliefs lie deeper in the unconscious mind. They reflect the way a child looks at the world, which is much closer to black and white. Look at a two-year-old screaming "I hate you!" to her mommy as she throws a tantrum in the supermarket, or the devastating loneliness of getting lost in a store when you are three, or the terror of going off to primary school the first day.

The inner child stays with you, buried beneath the adult layers, looking at the world in terms of stark doubts and fears.

Do I feel safe?
Is anybody my friend?
Does anyone love me?
Am I going to be abandoned?
Am I good enough?

The stark emotions these questions evoke reflect primal needs. If those needs are satisfied beginning in childhood, then you're more likely to hold on to the core belief "Life is good." If primal needs aren't fulfilled, you seize on opposite core beliefs associated with "Life is bad." How sad it is that the comforts of modern society are masking a widespread lack of fulfillment. It's very touching that people in the past who lived painfully primitive existences (from the viewpoint of iPads, penicillin, and jet travel) were able to adopt core beliefs, expressed through the rituals that permeated their lives, that were so life affirming.

They believed in a higher power that was the source of infinite love. They believed that suffering could be ended. They believed in eternal life. Looking back at Jerusalem at the time of Jesus or India at the time of Buddha, a skeptic might say, "No wonder they bought into promises about heaven or how much God loved them. When your life is spent scrabbling in the dirt, Nirvana sounds pretty sweet." But the truth is that without the rituals that reinforced their core beliefs, the inspiration to keep growing and evolving would have died out. None of us would be here without the faith that sustained our distant forebears, offering hope and promise.

We mentioned that Lori wasn't yet at the point where she had an "Aha" moment. But it did come one day. Her church group was helping preschoolers in a bad part of town with donated clothing, books, and toys. It was a cold, damp December just before the holidays.

"The kids were standing in line with their parents, a lot of whom looked ashamed to be there. The volunteers were acting as cheerful as we could be. One little girl came up to me, and I handed her a doll. She was so eager for it—I imagine she thought somebody would take it from her—that she snatched it out of my hand. She started to run away, hugging the doll. Suddenly she turned around and looked at me. Her eyes were big and shining, and in them I saw absolute love." It was a huge "Aha" for Lori.

It was as if someone were saying, "Lori, you are now good enough." In a glance of love she saw a life lesson. Love is everywhere, waiting to be expressed. It's the air our souls breathe. After that moment, she no longer looked back on her childhood as troubled. She saw things in a very different light. Everyone had been doing the best they could to love one another. Despite their failings and shortcomings, love had been shining through whenever it found an opening, using frail human beings as its vehicle.

Without the ritual of her church's annual giving campaign, Lori might never have had this experience. Rituals are the tools through which love is able to flow. They provide a structure for connection that enable each of us to discover ourselves.

Lori didn't go on to sell millions of books; that wasn't her path. Yet her breakthrough was just as valuable as Marci's. Her Life Design was beginning to become clear, and the decisive step had been when Lori chose to do what she loved. By showing kindness to herself, and to others, she was testing whether "Life is good" made more sense than "Life is bad." Whether people realize it or not, we all face the same choice at the level of our core beliefs.

An "Aha" moment clears up such double binds. You see that you are being pulled in opposite directions. We know a man who became infatuated with a woman who wasn't infatuated with him. "I can love you in other ways," she said, "but we'll never be intimate." They were already good friends, and she was being sincere. The man couldn't take it, however. He knew he would never love anyone else the way he loved her. So he started a campaign to win her over, showering her with gifts, leaving flowers on her desk at work, sending e-mails that were borderline suggestive, and lavishing her with attention as much as he could.

The woman never complained. She allowed his infatuated behavior to continue for several months. The man became more lovesick the more his wooing failed. Then one day a wise buddy told him, "You should lay off. It sounds like you're harassing her. That's abuse."

Shocked, the man ran to the woman and said, "You're always so nice to me. But do you think I'm abusing you?"

"Yes," she said.

"Why didn't you say so before?" he asked. "I was just trying to show how much I love you."

"I know," she replied with a smile. "Your weird behavior was just a blip on the screen. I love you anyway." At which point he broke down crying.

Looking back, the man sees this moment as a major turning point. Not only did he stop his harassing behavior, but he saw that love meant much more than he had ever imagined. It meant self-sacrifice, not putting your own desires ahead of those of someone you care about. More to the point, he realized the contradiction between "I love you" and "I have to get what I want." He was trying to make two opposites fit together, and they simply don't.

Everyone's life is blocked by inner contradictions. Love probably offers the most glaring examples. We say, "I love you," and truly mean it. But in another compartment of ourselves, we feel free to be selfish, to dump our garbage on the ones we love, to hurt their feelings, put them down, act domineering, and so on. Well, that's life, we say. Nobody's perfect. But the clash between love and ego stands for a deep contradiction, and until it's resolved, real love can't flourish.

GETTING TO "AHA"

Where will your breakthrough come from? It will come from something you deeply yearn for that has hit a wall. If what you yearn for means enough, you won't be able to tolerate being blocked. It is your passion, and nothing can keep you from it. There has to be a way to get over, around, or through the wall. At that point, your Life Design is guiding you, and unseen forces take charge. The unconscious mind plays its part, searching for an answer even when you aren't aware of it. At the same time, events start to move in an unexpected way.

During these times of challenge, the greatest opportunities exist for clearing the blocks that have kept you from accessing the love, power, and creativity at your spiritual core. Rituals create an anchor in these times of turbulence. At the same time, they allow the stress of these transitions to be released. After weathering a crisis, many people look back to find that they are stronger and less afraid.

The closer you get to your breakthrough, the more you will observe the following:

The pressure to change grows. You feel this as restlessness, or what a sage called "the flame of discontent."

You feel a mixture of longing in your dissatisfaction. There must be something more to life than this.

Old ways of behaving start to lose their appeal. Your life in general feels stale, or perhaps you see yourself at a dead end.

You worry that nothing will ever change, and yet you keep pushing for change.

This state could be called *fermentation*, when something new is starting to bubble up inside, like wine casks in spring fermenting from grape juice. Besides the inner signs of a psychological shift, there will be outer signs. People close to you will notice that you're somehow different (and most won't like it). Unforeseen opportunities will begin to appear, as if events are responding to your needs. There's no guarantee that you will reach liftoff; sometimes it takes repeated attempts before your confusion suddenly turns into clarity. This is one of the reasons why repetition is one of the prescriptions for effective rituals. But there is something about the most inspiring "Aha" moments that seem somehow predestined, because they reveal truths that are built into your Life Design. You rise above your everyday self, and with a rush of joy you know what it means to hear the angels sing.

The Light of Truth

Things you see when your Life Design emerges:

Life is filled with infinite possibilities.
Your every action serves you to evolve.
Everything is connected. Nothing is random or out of place.
You matter, and you have a unique contribution to make.

Everything you can see and touch is a mask, and behind the
mask is pure silence, peace, and creativity. Reality has its
home in that place.

You are loved, and the flow of this love is infinite, permeating
every aspect of existence.

You are at the center of creation.

These are beautiful truths, and one reason it takes an "Aha" moment to realize them is that everyday life runs by different rules. We don't see ourselves in the eternal flow of love when the roof leaks. The immediate task is not to get wet.

But you can shape everyday life to align with these truths. They will uphold you more and more as you grow. Nothing is more worthwhile, we feel, and we hope we've persuaded you to feel the same.

Now that you've gained a spectacular view of the territory, it's time to fulfill your dreams and wishes. The path of evolution moves forward by desire. So what do you desire? What area of your life cries out for change, improvement, and uplift? Whatever your answer is—and you may have many answers—the next part of this book will guide you through precise rituals fitted to the major areas of life, from family and relationships to wellness and wealth. Your hidden riches await!

Part Two

RITUALS *to* MEET *your* NEEDS

RITUALS FOR MAGICAL RELATIONSHIPS

The best love is the kind that awakens the soul;
that makes us reach for more,
that plants the fire in our hearts
and brings peace to our minds.

—FROM THE MOVIE *THE NOTEBOOK*

Oh, God! I'm forty-nine years old and still single. This isn't looking good. Am I ever going to find love? I'm not even dating! Am I over the hill?"

Emily was discouraged. She felt as if she'd never been in a long-term relationship that worked, or even had a prayer of becoming the permanent, committed soul connection she so dearly longed for. She was at a loss to explain why. She was attractive, and American men seemed to love her British accent. ("What's wrong with all these blokes anyway?" she'd ask herself.) She didn't even have a regular boyfriend!

Emily loved working at OPICA (Optimistic People In a Caring Atmosphere). The place had been her saving grace. Finding an intern position at this haven for the elderly who were dealing with dementia had happened quite by accident. Her internship turned into a full-time job, and the staff at OPICA were dear to her. If her heart overflowed with love for them, why couldn't it do the same for a man?

The guys she'd found either turned out to be total jerks, or somehow her own commitment fears would bubble up, and then the man got turned off and left her. Maybe she was just cursed.

Emily sighed. This whole relationship thing was driving her nuts, as her heart longed for an intimate connection with a man she could share her life with.

"You've got to call Dr. Sylva," her friend Denise said one day. "She's amazing, and I know she can help you get through this."

"Why not?" Emily thought. Nothing else was working.

When she made the call, Dr. Sylva's warmth and encouragement immediately put her at ease. "I understand how you're feeling," Sylva told her. "It's natural after so many disappointments to get discouraged. But there are some very easy, fun things you can do to change your experience." Emily found herself feeling better already.

"The key to changing your experience is first doing some mental and emotional housekeeping," Sylva said. She began to explain the use and purpose of rituals. "Ritual is a way to clean the corridors of your mind and the passageways of your heart so there's room for your guy to come in. Love needs an open space, and if your mind and heart are full of old emotions and expectations, you need to create that space."

Following Sylva's advice, Emily went to work on her housekeeping tasks. First, she wrote out all her unrequited feelings about Mark, the man she'd been fixated on but who wasn't interested in her, and once this was complete, she ripped the paper into tiny pieces and let the wind carry away all those old memories. Sylva explained that this ritual was a symbolic way of letting go of the past, and allowing her body, mind, and soul to know that she was ready for the new.

Next, Emily went to the beach with a girlfriend and screamed into the waves all the "gunk" she was ready to release: her frustration, resentment, anger, and sadness. When she felt completely cleansed, Emily sat with her friend and described the heartfelt intentions she was now accepting into her life. To ensure that Mark was no longer being held on to as a fantasy, Sylva assigned Emily the task of removing all traces of him, which meant deleting his Facebook photo and phone number along with any reminders of him lying around her apartment.

"We're making room in your life for the lover who hasn't shown up yet," Sylva told her. Already Emily was beginning to feel that he could show up. Her apartment had never experienced such a scrubbing. Boxes filled with the accumulated junk of years had been hauled out to the curb for the trash collector. At Sylva's urging, she literally made space for her new man, emptying a drawer for him, setting a place at the table, and making room for his things in the closet.

She also made a decision to consult the ancient Chinese rituals of feng shui in order to make her space conducive to a new relationship. Since her bathroom turned out to be her relationship corner, according to the consultant, she bought red towels (symbolic of love) and made sure she had two of everything in the bathroom. The Matisse print on the wall was now adorned with a photo of George Clooney, across which Emily had written in bold letters, "Alone no more!!"

Now that she had cleared out the past physically, mentally, emotionally, and spiritually, Emily went on to the next stage of making her intention as definite as possible. Sylva took her through the Strategic Attraction planning process taught by Jan Stringer and Alan Hickman (www.thehiddenriches.com/attraction). This four-part process was aimed at getting Emily crystal clear about the qualities and characteristics of the man she wanted to be with—what made him tick; what she wanted him to expect of her as a lover, a friend, and a partner; and what would make her attractive to him.

At first Emily felt reticent to write down *everything* she wanted in a man. After all, most of these things were like frosting on the cake, but it turned out to be really fun, and finally she decided just to go for it and write down everything she could possibly think of. What could it hurt? Later she said that this experience had been mind-blowing. What a revelation to realize that she could ask for what she really wanted! Of course, this didn't mean that there weren't some lingering doubts, but overall it was an incredible step for her. The texture of her rituals became richer and richer. She created a Vision Book, in which she pasted photos and created descriptions that expressed her ideal life with a man. They represented what their relationship would be like, and how she would feel in such a relationship.

It wasn't all vision, however. From her Strategic Attraction Plan, Emily knew she wanted her man to feel physically attracted to her. To help that along, she began Pilates classes and a steady workout routine. Sylva told her that if she wanted to meet her ideal man, she would have to get out of the house regularly. So Emily began her weekly "out and about" ritual. Each week she would do something outside the house that was fun for her. Whether it was meeting a friend at a local café, going out dancing, or joining in an excursion, she was with other people at least once a week.

When you stand back and look at Emily's new program, you'll see it's very different from the one that millions of single women in her position are used to. Their approach consists of a lot of waiting around for the phone to ring, going out only with girlfriends (most of the time spent complaining about men, why the good ones are all taken, etc.), and living with a cat. None of these helps activate the movement of life energy. Emily found herself becoming much more energized and optimistic. Every new ritual made her feel better about herself, more in control, and more open about what her true intentions were.

Sylva talked to her about the power of visualization, telling her stories about Olympic gold medalists in gymnastics who visualized performing their routine to a perfect score of 10, and about prisoners of war who kept themselves alive by visualizing themselves in a situation back home that made their hearts sing. Emily began her own daily visualization ritual. Each morning she'd sit for a few minutes listening to her favorite love songs and visually imagining her life with the man of her dreams. Sylva encouraged her to use all her senses, to hear, touch, and feel him in her life. Emily especially loved this routine. Not only did it fill her heart with love and joy, but she began to feel hopeful that her vision could really become a reality.

Soon Emily began meeting some candidates she considered promising, but after a few dates, each got crossed off the list. Whenever she started to become discouraged, Sylva let her know that these experiences were a sign that she was getting closer. Having someone who was in her corner like this, supporting her each step of the way, really helped Emily's confidence. The key, Sylva said, was to keep her attention on what she was choosing to create, not on what she didn't want.

Then one cold February day, almost a year after her first session with Sylva, Emily met Larry. As part of her weekly "out and about" excursions she would join her girlfriend Mel at the Golden Mean Café in Los Angeles. The month before, Mel had met a man at a workshop whom she really liked. Larry was a great guy, but Mel could tell he'd lost heart and given up hope of finding a special woman to share his life with. For some reason, he wasn't for her, but Mel told him about her wonderful, gorgeous girlfriends. She thought surely one of them would feel a soul connection with Larry.

Was he open to meeting them? "Absolutely!" was his enthusiastic response.

Pulling into the parking lot of the café where Larry would be waiting, Emily watched as a tall, bearlike guy (the kind she found superattractive) walked in front of her car. "Wow! I hope that's him," she thought. Going inside, she saw the same guy giving Mel a big hug. "That *is* him!" she realized. Whether it was all the rituals Emily had been doing or not, that day Emily was the only one of Mel's girlfriends to show up.

Her first impressions were just right. "I was struck by how easy he was to be with and talk to. His heart was huge and his attitude so positive, he was a bright light to be around."

Larry's description of her was even more dramatic. "I was entranced by this woman. As we talked, it was as if there were this arc of electricity passing between us. I can't begin to tell you how disappointed I was when it turned out that she had another commitment for the night of the concert I invited her to."

Larry wasn't about to let that stop him. He got Emily's phone number, and the next day he asked if she'd have dinner with him the following week. Emily describes the evening: "It was magical. I had been on so many blah Internet dates, and this one was a huge relief. Because Mel knew Larry and felt so good about him, I was able to completely relax and melt into the attention he showered on me."

Larry wrote to Sylva about six months after he and Emily met. "I am the man who has fallen in love with Emily. Perhaps a better way of saying this is, I am the man who showed up when you and Emily had done the hard work of clearing, purging, and manifesting me!" Six months later he and Emily moved in together.

They have continued to grow in love and are now engaged. Like any couple they have ups and downs, yet they both know the importance of choosing where to put their attention so that they are focusing on the positives instead of the negatives in their relationship.

Whether you're still looking for that special person to share your life with or you're already in an established relationship, the rituals below will help you create something rich, fulfilling, and enduring, the kind of relationship that Emily and Larry have begun so successfully.

RITUAL PRACTICE

Attracting the Perfect Partner

If you don't yet have that special relationship in your life, and deeply want it, try the steps that Sylva shared with Emily and see what happens. Below is a summary. These rituals will also work if you want to improve the relationship you're already in. In the list below, we've *italicized* our suggestions for adapting these to your existing relationship. If there are no italicized additions, use that item as it is.

Most people think that if they're unhappy in a marriage, their partner has to change. The truth is, when you change, the world around you changes as well. So, if you want to make your marriage better, start by redefining what that relationship is inside you. Remember, what you put your attention on grows stronger in your life!

1. Write out all your negative feelings about your past relationship(s), then rip the paper into tiny pieces and let

the wind carry all those old, stale memories away. *(For an existing relationship, write out all your negative feelings about this relationship up until now.)*

2. Find a beach, a mountaintop, or somewhere with wide-open spaces, then scream into the waves, the mountains, etc., all the "gunk" you are now releasing.

3. Sit with a friend and describe the heartfelt desires and intentions you are now accepting into your life. *(This is the time to get really clear about what you want your relationship to be if you're already in one.)*

4. Remove all traces of your past relationships from your life. *(Remove any reminders of the negative associations in your existing relationship.)*

5. Begin making room in your life for the lover who is not yet here, but who you are beginning to feel could soon show up. *(For an existing relationship, this means making room emotionally. Start paying attention to all the good things your partner does and acknowledge them for those things. If it's hard to see any good things at first, aim to find at least one thing each day you can appreciate in your partner.)*

6. Receive a consultation in the ancient ritual of feng shui to make your space conducive to your new relationship.

7. Make space for your as yet invisible beloved, setting aside drawer space for him/her, setting a place for him/her at your table, making room in the closet for his/her things. *(As with 5, focus on making space in your heart for the partner you choose to have, even if he or she doesn't appear like that to you just yet. Make a point of making more time in your life for your partner as well.)*

8. Go through the Strategic Attraction planning process taught by Jan Stringer and Alan Hickman (www.thehiddenriches.com/attraction).

9. Write down *everything* you want in your man or woman.

10. Create a Vision Book to put into pictures the vision of your life with your soul mate, what your relationship would be like, and how you would feel in that relationship.

11. Get yourself out of the house. Each week do something that is fun for you.

12. Find exercise that you really enjoy, whether it's Pilates, cycling, running, Zumba, or whatever, and start working out regularly.

13. Begin your own daily visualization ritual. Each day listen to your favorite love songs, imagining your life with the man or woman of your dreams. Use all of your senses, to see and feel him/her in your life. *(For an existing relationship, gather together all the photos, mementos, and other items that remind you of good times you've had together. Create a space with these things around you and visualize your relationship as you choose it to be. Use all of your senses, as well as your feelings, as your partner becomes your perfect lover and soul mate in your mind's eye.)*

14. Take your life off hold. Start taking the trips you've dreamed about.

15. Now let go. Surrender. And see what the universe has in store for you.

LOVE AND YOUR LIFE DESIGN

Love is the glue that binds differences together, creating unity out of the diversity of life. The power of love permeates every level of your Life Design. If it's blocked, however, even partially, the power of love can't be felt in your inner and outer experience.

That's why the love in intimate relationships is so important. Two people often fall in love but then wind up in a troubled relationship down the line because issues around work, money, or sex become very difficult. Why wasn't love enough?

Because life energy runs through every aspect of existence, your Life Design is a complex tapestry reflecting your whole life and purpose. In some aspects there will be clarity because the energy flows freely. In other aspects the energy will be blocked, which leads to a distorted reflection. It is very valuable for both people in a relationship to see this. Alignment with your Life Design allows you and your spouse or partner to work toward the same goal—not the goal of getting your way or giving in instead, but the goal of smoothing the flow of life for both of you. The power of rituals is in spontaneously creating alignment with your Life Design. You don't have to think excessively about your purpose and role in life. These emerge naturally when you connect with your transcendent center at the spiritual core of your life.

As you clear the blocks that have prevented you from experiencing this connection, the contrast is immediate and dramatic. We'll use Emily and the five areas of inner life from the Life Design as an example.

Bliss As Emily cleared away the debris of her past disappointments and replaced it with what she chose to create, she grew happier. She became optimistic; she could see the possibility of having what her heart longed for. The bliss at the center of her Life Design started to shine through, infusing her interactions with other people, who in turn found her more attractive.

Knowingness When Emily first met Larry, she immediately felt at ease; as she was drawn to him, a part of her "knew" that something good was unfolding. A week later, when they had dinner together, this knowingness grew into a sense of peace and comfort with this man.

Mind On the level of mind, including emotions, Emily had to overcome the obstacles of past memories. She also worked on her old negative beliefs. Emotionally she took steps to transform her discouragement and pessimism into the kind of feelings she wanted her soul mate to experience in her. Mental obstacles also had the effect of denying her access to the levels of bliss and knowingness. She had gone on too many ill-advised first dates because she was disconnected from herself, and without doing conscious work beforehand, Larry easily could have been someone she would ignore or not connect with.

Energetic Emily's "stuff" was preventing her love from shining through in its full vibrancy. Sylva noticed Emily's barely concealed unhappiness at their first meeting, and any potential suitors would surely feel it as well. Having turned her listless energy into inner vitality, Emily sensed that her meeting with Larry was electric. This was so tangible that he remembers it to this day.

Material Form Although it was happening invisibly, Emily was changing her body chemistry as she changed her beliefs, attitudes, thoughts, and feelings. This deserves a little further explanation. According to a number of researchers, repressed emotions are stored in our cells as "molecules of emotion," a phrase coined by Dr. Candace Pert. These chemicals alter the flow of the body's information network. Negative messages impair the immune system, altering our moods and draining our energy. Even the output of genes is altered.

Life energy doesn't want to be blocked. It's very useful that mind, body, emotions, and spirit are intimately connected. You change one, and it will affect all the others. When Emily did the mental exercise of writing out the painful memories, fears, and beliefs she was holding on to, and followed this with the physical act of tearing the paper up, she created a shift in all of these interconnected areas.

Just making a start in your own life at removing similar blockages will have some effect. But one of the reasons repetition is part of ritual practice is regular reinforcement, which promotes permanent change. Emily's steady commitment to her process, staying regular with her rituals, in time paid off beautifully.

FORGIVENESS AND LETTING GO

Next, the story of a woman who woke up one morning with the oddest idea. "I think I forgot to get married."

At the time, Arielle Ford was forty-three and a huge success as a public relations agent. She had helped launch the career of Deepak Chopra, along with Jack Canfield and Mark Victor Hansen, co-creators of the *Chicken Soup for the Soul*® series, and Neale Donald Walsch, author of *Conversations with God*. Her list of prominent clients had gone on to include Wayne Dyer, Marianne Williamson, Louise Hay, and many others. She had a great Southern California lifestyle by the ocean, working with people she loved—Arielle was happy. But she had forgotten to get married.

Now she realized that the getting-married thing was actually important to her. But why? She considered herself past the age of having children, so it wasn't that. Some part of her was yearning for the connection, the love and affection of an intimate relationship in which both people are fully committed. Through her work with spiritual luminaries Arielle had been exposed to ways of manifesting her desires. She had gotten really good at using self-help tools. She would use her knowledge to manifest this newfound desire, too.

Arielle's situation looks very similar to Emily's, but she wasn't a newcomer to rituals, and she also had a good basis in self-knowledge. She looked inside and immediately spotted that her main obstacle had to do with holding on and lack of forgiveness. These would be her primary focus in the beginning. (At the same time she followed rituals similar to those we outlined in Emily's story.) Arielle looked back at a long string of soured relationships and saw a lot that needed forgiving, if she could find a way. There was resentment, hurt, and in some cases lasting bitterness, either toward herself or toward a previous lover. So she sat down and started making a list. Who were all the past lovers she still held some judgment about—was he a creep or a liar, whose traits had taken time to discover? Did he turn out to be selfish, or had he betrayed her? She dredged up the men in her past, and one by one she wrote them a letter.

Every letter was for herself, not the men. These were ritual letters, so Arielle didn't need to send them. Her purpose was to put down on paper everything that needed to be forgiven and released once and for all. She made a point to fully describe her own part in the breakdown of the relationship. She ended each letter with the words that expressed her conscious intent: "I forgive you, I love you, and I now release you."

In some cases when she wrote these words, she couldn't yet forgive and release her need to blame. For these men she erased the sentence and gave herself more time to consider how that person had helped her learn a valuable lesson or had served her in some other way. When she was really able to forgive and release him, then and only then did she add those words at the bottom of her letter.

The next step was to write a second letter for each lover, only this time it was addressed to her from him. Using her imagination, she put herself in the man's shoes and wrote down what the relationship had been like from his perspective. How had she hurt or frustrated him? Where had she been too controlling or had insisted unreasonably on getting her own way? She ended each letter with the same words, except this time he forgave and released her.

Once she was done, Arielle felt as if a huge weight had been lifted from her. She was no longer carrying all her old lovers around with her, and it was time to figure out who she wanted to replace them with. You've already read the rituals that Emily followed for making space for her ideal lover. Arielle added a few twists. The traits she wanted in the perfect man, for instance, included generosity, not only with money but with time, affection, and energy. He must absolutely love women and enjoy being with one. (Interestingly, Arielle was generous enough to add that he should love his mother and that his mother would be a great mother-in-law. She didn't want to compete with a rival for his affections. There was room for both, since her perfect man had a big heart.)

Because she was well aware of the power of ritual, Arielle was painstaking and detailed in listing exactly what she wanted (down to "He must be able to walk unassisted"!). But she had also learned something from her ritual of forgiving and releasing. She couldn't fixate on her desired qualities and become too attached to them.

"If I was too attached," Arielle says, "my chances of finding the perfect man would be reduced, not made better."

This is a key aspect of rituals—once you've performed them correctly and fully, you let go of your intention. This allows life to play out the unexpected sequence of events that brings someone what she most desires. The perfect man doesn't arrive on track 23 at 5:13 p.m. There has to be the element of spontaneity, being open and alert as your intention finds its unique path to fulfillment. Setbacks can turn into hidden steps forward—this happens quite often—and disappointments are symptoms of impatience.

Having made her list, reviewing it many times until she practically knew it by heart, she decided that this step needed its own ritual of release. Arielle looked for the next new moon, because she knew that in many traditional cultures, this was a good time for beginning new things. On the appointed day, she went to the beach and sat with her list. She closed her eyes and said a deep, heartfelt prayer of gratitude for the amazing man who was already being drawn into her life. Then she burned the list and scattered the ashes to the wind.

Since release opens blocked channels, allowing for the experience of bliss, a celebration was called for. Arielle drove to her favorite restaurant for a special lunch and a glass of champagne. She toasted her perfect man (in her mind's eye he was sitting across the table from her): "My love, I'm thrilled you are on your way. The cosmic welcome mat is out for you. Feel free to arrive at any time. I trust in perfect timing and your appearance in my life."

It's important to be aware that the finest level of feeling is essential in rituals for creating whatever you deeply wish for. This doesn't mean indulging in dramatic emotions with tears, pleading, breathless anticipation, and the ups and downs of histrionics. At the finest level you are drawing near the transcendent center of your Life Design. Here, feelings are quiet, certain, and harmonious, like bliss itself. In a word, your feelings are bathed in a soft light at the very edge of invisibility.

Arielle cultivated this subtle level of awareness. Every afternoon she would sit and feel in herself what a magical relationship would be like. She wasn't waiting for a man to give her those feelings. He would be blending with an experience that comes from within.

One day Arielle was asked to attend an important business meeting in northern California for one of her clients. She flew up and arrived a little early. As she was chatting with her client, Brian walked into the room, and the world stopped. As Arielle describes it now, "I knew, Brian knew, and everyone else in the room knew, too." (Brian later revealed that for three weeks before that fateful day, he had been dreaming that his soul mate was coming. The night before they met he saw her face clearly in a dream. So when he set eyes on Arielle, he recognized her instantly—this is a great example of what we'll talk about later, the power of the unseen parts of life.) Three weeks later they were engaged, and a year later they got married. In 2013, they celebrated their fifteenth wedding anniversary.

THE TOOTHPASTE TUBE

As much as Arielle loved Brian, there were times when their life together wasn't Shangri-La. As with the toothpaste tube. All her life she had carefully rolled the toothpaste up from the bottom as it got used. The toothpaste was always there at the end where it came out; this only made sense.

But Brian was a free, easygoing spirit. He would grab the toothpaste and squeeze it onto his toothbrush without worrying about pinching the middle of the tube or losing the last bit at the bottom. Every time Arielle walked into the bathroom and saw the toothpaste tube scrunched up, she'd have a moment when steam started coming out of her ears. "Why can't he do it right?" It was such a reasonable request, yet no amount of coaxing, explaining, or reminding seemed to make any difference. Brian would just shrug his shoulders with a quizzical expression on his face and go about his life.

The toothpaste tube got Arielle to thinking about *wabi-sabi*, the ancient Japanese way of approaching life that finds the perfect in the imperfect. For example, in a Japanese museum holding a precious antique porcelain vase, if the vase has a large crack running through it, a light would be directed to highlight the crack, which has become part of the design and the vase's overall beauty (the way a small mole on a lovely woman's face can be characterized as a beauty mark). It is out of wabi-sabi that the 1,200-year-old Japanese tea ceremony was created.

Arielle had practiced wabi-sabi in other parts of her life, but after enough scrunched toothpaste tubes, she found herself standing in front of Brian, hand on hip, wagging a finger in his face. Suddenly she had an insight. She realized that she was reproducing behavior she had watched in her mother the whole time she was growing up. She shared her insight with Brian and asked him to do her a favor. "Whenever I start in like this, will you just say, 'When did Sheila [Arielle's mom] enter the room?'"

This exchange helped Brian realize that he sometimes repeated behavior picked up from his dad, Wayne. So he asked Arielle to say, "Oh, I just noticed, Wayne has joined us."

But the toothpaste tube still proved a bit recalcitrant. Try as she might, Arielle couldn't see the perfection in Brian's habit of squeezing the middle of the tube. Finally it came to her. She was married to a man who always brushes his teeth. What a gift! That meant she could enjoy kissing him; he was more likely to keep his teeth; and she didn't have to deal with bad breath. The scrunched tube was a reminder of how unique Brian was in her life. Arielle summarizes her experience: "We've been brainwashed by society into seeking some idyllic state where two beautiful people are all smiles all the time. That kind of perfection is really pure fiction. When your partner is imperfect, but you can find perfection in that, you will have the best chance for a long, affectionate, and fulfilling love affair."

Today, Arielle has shared her remarkable experiences in her books *The Soulmate Secret* and *Wabi Sabi Love*. Here's a ritual based on her teachings that you can start using now:

RITUAL PRACTICE

Wabi-Sabi

Begin to practice wabi-sabi in your own life. Seeing the perfection in imperfection takes a while to burn into your neural pathways, but this practice is invaluable if you're committed to living a happy, joyful life. Take a few minutes each day to reconsider one or two things that are irritating, frustrating, or upsetting in your relationship. How can you find the perfection in them? The challenge is about changing your perspective without demanding change from your partner.

On a piece of paper (or better yet, a journal) draw a vertical line down the middle. On the left-hand side note the thing that upsets you. On the right-hand side write down the gift you received from it, the perfection being brought out. One by one the things about your partner that really bug you will be included.

This ritual takes imagination and the willingness to release your "stuff." As with Arielle and the toothpaste tube, some concepts you hold about how the world should run will make it hard to see the gift at first. Just keep at it. If you really get stuck, you can ask for help from your spouse or a friend.

To get you started, here are a few examples. The gifts we suggest are just possibilities, not the way you have to think:

A. He's messy and you're a neatnik. Seeing dirty dishes in the sink and socks tossed on the floor offends your sense of tidiness.

The gift: Those socks remind me of my need to be in control and how that often doesn't serve me. Those dirty dishes remind me that we have been amply provided with food and have a place to put our dirty dishes.

B. He stays glued to video games and ignores you.

The gift: I can play a game, too. I'll keep buying lingerie and walk across the room until the perfect one makes it impossible for him to stick with Nintendo. He's a kid at heart, and that's something I really love in him. It brings out the fun in me and arouses my caring streak.

C. She flirts with other men at parties.

The gift: Smile to yourself as you think, "Buddy, I'm the one she's going home with." Consider how lucky you are to have someone so attractive that others can't help but be drawn to her.

Keep up the discipline of doing this ritual for at least a month, and you will begin to see the hint of perfection in every situation, no matter how challenging it may appear at first.

SEXUALITY AND RELATIONSHIPS

Sex. We all want it. We all seek it. Yet sex is a source of confusion and worry for many. Physical intimacy can become fulfilling or frustrating for anyone. Sex manuals by the dozen won't help if your life energy is blocked. Sex turns the flow of energy into a flood—that's how it should feel—that settles the mind, warmly spreads through the body, and brings excitement to the emotions. We spoke before about how inner distortions in the Life Design can spill over into distorted behavior in outer life. This is nowhere more true than with sexual frustration (or in extreme cases, sexual pathology), which can lead otherwise balanced people to do reckless things. Since the beginning of time, ancient cultures have developed rituals that allow a person to control the fuming volcano of sexual energy and direct it into ecstatic experiences.

When Janet first met Marie and Nathan more than twenty years ago, she told Marie, "I want a relationship just like yours and Nathan's. You guys are bonded at the hip, and you're the happiest couple I've ever met."

Marie started laughing. "As a matter of fact, in terms of compatibility, we have some incredible mismatches—a lot more, I imagine, than couples who should never be together at all."

"Then what makes you two seem so totally connected?" Janet asked. "What's the deal?"

Marie began telling Janet about an earlier, more troubled time. She had come out of a failed marriage and was alone for several years. She became depressed and doubtful that she would be able to have a successful relationship. Marie was sometimes too anxious even to let the subject of relationships enter her mind. Wasn't every couple she knew struggling with some kind of disappointment?

"I was now a single mother of three, working in migrant education. But the job was helping me deal with my own problems. It was the beginning of my branching out and seeing the needs of people on the fringes of society."

Around this time, Marie learned to meditate, and instead of viewing her life as a failure, she began to change.

"One part of my job was to go into homes we called 'chicken shacks' because they were so run down and decrepit. That's when I learned to appreciate the challenges migrant workers faced. My challenges faded away by comparison.

"Then I remembered a verse from the Old Testament, *'I will restore the years that the locusts have eaten.'* I started to feel more hopeful about the possibility of finding love and support with another person. Maybe those years of disappointment and heartache that 'the locusts' had eaten away could be restored. Right around that time I met Nathan."

On their first date, Nathan and Marie went to a restaurant and wound up talking for a long time. What she estimated was only an hour turned out to be over three. "All of a sudden I understood the saying about time standing still," says Marie, looking back wistfully on their glorious beginning.

The relationship quickly moved to the stage of physical intimacy. A mutual friend gave them information about "Tantric lovemaking," as he called it. Tantra is from the Vedic tradition of India. What Marie and Nathan were actually given, it turned out, were notes from a course by Dr. Stephen Chang, the author and creator of *The Tao of Sexology,* based on an ancient Chinese tradition.

"For fifteen minutes in the evening Nathan and I read from the notes, and it was apparent to us that a completely new world of sexual possibility had opened up for us. After we read a passage, Nathan would say, 'Now it's time for the laboratory part of the course.' Following Dr. Chang's advice about making love was so much fun, we both were completely into it. We discovered that a set of simple rituals can have a profound effect on the feelings of intimacy we experienced being together."

Despite their previous relationships, they were learning for the first time the real meaning of loving intimacy.

"One evening I said to Nathan, 'Let's be really married.' Through Dr. Chang's course, I had come to realize what marriage really meant in terms of merging your energies. It was something precious, sacred, and powerful. I wanted that." Central to the Chinese tradition is the balance of yin and yang, or in this case male and female sexual energy, to achieve wholeness. Opposites in nature may seem to be separate or even clashing with each other. In truth, they are complementary. The balancing of yin and yang in a relationship involves many aspects, such as supporting one another emotionally, respecting the differences inherent in male and female, and sharing equally the act of making love.

Rituals for sexual intercourse can transform an ordinary relationship into an extraordinary one. It takes work on the part of both partners, as Nathan and Marie discovered.

"When the balance point is hit between two lovers, you are touching transcendence, the source of existence. The sexual practices we learned were all for the purpose of creating a feeling of 'going beyond,' which is what 'transcendence' means. It's a feeling of unity or oneness that can't be described in words.

"Dr. Chang taught many exercises for women and others for men. One pair he called the female deer and the male deer exercise [Note: For instructions on doing these particular exercises, go to www.thehiddenriches.com/relationships].

"The female deer exercise was to calm a woman's energy and the male deer exercise was to balance the man's energy and strengthen his prostate so that he could have intercourse without ejaculating.

With sufficient control, the man could have intimate relations for a couple of hours and then ejaculate." In Chinese medicine they say the soft overcomes the hard. Oftentimes the woman's sexual energy is so powerful that it will draw an ejaculation out of the man. Then he has no choice but to find release, unless, that is, he's learned something like the male deer exercise.

Sexual rituals are designed to create intimacy. When you treat them as special, they will be special. Have a formal beginning to the intimate sessions when the two of you together light candles, put on some music, and take a few minutes perhaps to share what you appreciate about each other. As you see the good in your partner, and your partner expresses the good he or she sees in you, both of you will feel drawn to each other—the rest becomes automatic.

Marie continues, "In the morning Nathan and I would do our exercises separately. Then we'd come together, naked, skin to skin. Contact isn't just erotic. They say when a premature baby is born, the best chance it has of living and thriving is by putting it right on the mother's skin. It's called 'kangaroo care.'

"Two people lying together naked experience the same nourishing sense of closeness that is so crucial for the survival of a newborn baby.

"Because of this new type of lovemaking, Nathan and I learned to relax into each other's energy. Once we were able to relax, he would have an erection. The erection was without a lot of urging or frantic activity or worrying about whether anything would happen or not."

To set lovemaking apart from all the other activities in your life, don't just get up and go on with something else after you finish. Bring this beautiful time together to a formal close. After holding each other for a while, you can create a formal close by putting out the candles together as you each share a few things you're grateful for in your relationship. When you plan a few minutes at the beginning and end of sex, you create a "sacred space" within which your intimacy will be enhanced.

"We also practiced an exercise Dr. Chang called morning and evening prayer. It's pretty simple. The couple lies together, naked, in the morning and/or evening. Using a little stimulation or with lubricant, the man enters the woman. Then with just enough movement so that the man maintains his erection, the couple put their mouths together and breathe back and forth.

"You might think, 'How do you get enough oxygen when you're breathing into your partner's mouth?' But you do. During this exercise there is no intent to achieve orgasm or to engage in full lovemaking. It's all about intimacy. This exercise was one of the most powerful we found in creating a deep sense of connection between us.

"It was a coming together without a lot of motion. There would be shallow penetration at first, then deeper penetration, using just a little bit of movement, enough to keep the erection going. And because we would do this often, our energy became harmonious and balanced, while our lovemaking grew into something indescribable. This exercise taught us to be more than our separate selves, focused solely on our individual pleasure."

Marie concluded, "For years these practices have bound us together more deeply than I could ever have hoped. We continue to follow the Tao of Sexology, and I strongly recommend it for any couple who want to open up new horizons of intimacy."

The sexual revolution has had many consequences, but one of the saddest may be the way that divorcing couples say they've simply grown apart. There's a lot more sex being openly discussed and yet not nearly enough intimacy. Ancient cultures around the world have recognized the central role that sexual intercourse plays in creating enduring connections. The whole realm of sexual energy and creating oneness was fully explored. Whatever the tradition, the core of this knowledge is the creation of balance between male and female so that sexual energy can be directed upward through the heart and spiritual centers of the body. The value of this understanding leaves modern sex manuals in the dust. Nothing replaces personal experience and the desire for transformation, which sexual intimacy can fulfill for both partners once they are as open to it as Marie and Nathan.

RITUAL PRACTICE

For Intimacy

We strongly recommend the morning and evening prayer exercise that Marie described above. For a ritual directly related to sexual energy, try the following:

Sit naked together with your partner, facing each other. Put your right hand on their heart center, in the center of their chest, while they do the same with you. Each of you put your left hand on your navel center, right over your belly button. Now take turns sharing one thing you appreciate about the other and why you love that about them. By saying why you appreciate someone, and if you speak from a level of real feeling, it will go deeper and be more meaningful.

Continue until you can't resist taking each other in your arms and making love.

Because this is a PG-rated book, we will not describe some of the powerful sexual practices couples can do to create intimacy and connection. Instead, we recommend you get a copy of Dr. Stephen Chang's book *The Tao of Sexology*. There you will find very practical, useful, and effective rituals you and your partner can practice to transform your experience of being in a relationship.

Relationship is ultimately about your growth as a whole. When all the gates of your inner life are open, you are deeply connected to your core—what we call your "transcendent center." From that place, at the center of your life, the gifts that emerge are breathtaking. The most precious of these is the way that love begins to permeate every part of your existence.

RITUALS FOR DIET, HEALTH, AND BEAUTY

It's a tradition at Saddleback Church in Lake Forest, California. Pastor Rick Warren, Saddleback's senior pastor, was baptizing 858 people. Baptism is a full-immersion ritual at the church he founded, now one of the largest mega-churches in America. On this day it took four hours, and afterward Pastor Rick told his congregation that somewhere around the five hundredth person, he had the thought, "We're all fat." More personally he thought, "I'm fat. I'm a terrible model. I can't expect our people to get in shape unless I do."

Rick Warren is the author of *The Purpose Driven Life*, which has sold close to thirty-five million copies. Saddleback Church has some 30,000 members and ten campuses scattered across Southern California. Pastor Rick is not one to do things in a small way. This would be no exception.

Around the same time that Pastor Rick was confronting his congregation's part in America's fast-spreading obesity epidemic, Dr. Daniel Amen woke up to a beautiful, sunny Sunday morning. He was also a celebrated author who had just finished his latest book, *The Amen Solution: The Brain Healthy Way to Get Thinner, Smarter, Happier,* and he was feeling great. That Sunday Amen and his wife, Tana, decided to visit a new church near their home. The parking lot was jammed, and Amen went to get seats while his wife took their young daughter to the children's service. Walking toward the sanctuary, he passed tables of doughnuts being sold for charity. Since he had warned in his books about how toxic food adversely affects the brain, he found the sugary mounds of carbohydrates really irritating. Past the doughnuts were hot grills full of bacon and sausage, then hundreds of hot dogs being prepared for after the service.

Amen settled into a pew, and the minister began by complimenting everyone who had helped with an ice cream social held the night before. The health-conscious doctor was doubly irritated now. When his wife arrived, she saw her husband typing furiously into his smartphone. She shot him a sharp look, so he tilted the screen for her to see. It read,

> Go to church . . . get doughnuts . . . bacon . . . sausage . . . hot dogs . . . ice cream. They have no idea they are sending people to heaven early!

Amen spent the rest of the service praying that somehow God would give him the means to change places of worship, no matter what the religion, so that part of their mission was to help worshippers become stewards of their bodies. Modifying self-destructive behavior was his specialty, since Amen's training had been in psychiatry (the *Washington Post* once called him "the most popular psychiatrist in America"). From a medical perspective, he was acutely aware of the link between such foods as doughnuts, fatty meats, and white bread and a higher risk of contracting heart disease, type 2 diabetes, and other chronic illnesses. Amen and Pastor Rick were following parallel tracks.

Two weeks later Amen got a call from Steve Komanapalli, the assistant pastor at Saddleback Church, asking if Amen could meet with Pastor Rick about a new initiative at the church called Decade of Destiny. After his realization during the baptism ceremony, Warren's staff was putting together a ten-year program to help their congregation become healthy in every aspect of life, including the physical. Clearly someone had been listening to the good doctor's prayer (those "unseen" parts of life at work again).

When they met, Pastor Warren, who is six feet two and at that time was topping the scales at around 300 pounds, asked about a catchphrase of Amen's, "Dinosaur syndrome: Big body, little brain, become extinct." This was a term Amen coined after reading about the research of another physician, Dr. Cyrus Raji at the University of Pittsburgh. Raji found that as weight goes up, the actual physical size of the brain goes down. Obese people had eight percent less brain tissue, and their brains looked sixteen years older than the brains of lean people. Being overweight also doubles your risk for Alzheimer's disease.

Before, the evidence that being overweight can shorten one's life span had never made an impact on Pastor Rick. For one thing, he was a man of God, and dying held no fear for him. When anyone teased him that he would be sexier if he were thinner, he would just laugh, "I'm already sexy enough!" But when he heard that if he didn't lose weight, he'd be dumber, *that* made an impact.

Amen and the pastor talked about Rick's diet. "I'm not hungry until two in the afternoon," he said. "I could fast until noon every day of the week, but then my appetite kicks in, and I eat big amounts of food until late at night."

"You have to change your eating pattern," Amen warned. "Study after study has shown that people who eat breakfast are more likely to lose weight and keep it off. By eating regularly, you keep your blood sugar more stable throughout the day. Stable blood sugar wards off cravings. It doesn't just help weight loss; it also sharpens your focus, memory, and decision-making skills."

At this point in the story, we'd like to underline that one of the greatest benefits of establishing foundation rituals in your daily routine is keeping healthy. Your body *loves* routine. The more regular you are in going to bed and getting up in the morning, exercising, mealtimes, and twice-daily meditation or prayer, the healthier the effect on your body will be. (And of course these daily rituals also deliver the time, energy, and orderly mind benefits we talked about in the first chapter, "A Vision of Fulfillment.") Here's the key: your body cannot be healthy without considering how to make your whole life healthy.

There is no escaping how the mind and body are interconnected. The spiritual dimension is also part of the connection—that's the realization Rick Warren made, seeing that his spiritual ministry should include physical health. At its core, every faith considers the human body sacred, a temple to be revered and cared for.

At their first meeting, Amen advised Pastor Rick that to create real change in his congregation he would have to buy into the concept personally, on a deep emotional level, that if you overeat, you're not being a good steward of your body. In a word, doughnuts were out.

"But we built this church on doughnuts!" the pastor wailed. Amen knew he had his work cut out for him.

For decades churches have relied on social functions to bring people together and keep them connected to the church. Potlucks, ice cream socials, pizza parties, barbecues, pancake breakfasts, spaghetti dinners—and doughnuts—have become part of what it means to "go to church." Over the next three months Amen, the Saddleback staff, and the other physicians who had signed on developed "the Daniel Plan." It wasn't named after Daniel Amen but rather the biblical Daniel in the Old Testament, who was taken into captivity in Babylon as a young man. He refused to eat the fatty rich meat and flowing wine offered to him as a privileged captive in King Nebuchadnezzar's court, sustaining himself instead on vegetables and water. To everyone's astonishment, after ten days Daniel looked healthier and better nourished than any of the other young slaves.

With Scripture behind it, the Daniel Plan was launched at a large public rally in January 2011. It's a fifty-two-week program grounded in the 5,000 Bible study groups that already existed in the Saddleback congregation. Amen says this is the secret that makes the plan so effective. Everyone needs a support system to make meaningful change. These small groups created a collective commitment to help one another get healthy.

From the start, the Daniel Plan was an instant hit. So many people wanted to attend the kickoff rally that thousands were turned away. On the first day 9,200 people signed up. Today more than 15,000 have gone through the program, collectively shedding more than 270,000 pounds of excess weight.

RITUAL PRACTICE

The Daniel Plan

When Pastor Rick Warren told his congregation the keys to his losing sixty pounds in the first year of the Daniel Plan, he attributed it to:

Meaning—Ritual is effective when it is connected to something deeply meaningful to *you*. The Daniel Plan helped Warren frame his eating, exercise, and health plans as a spiritual discipline, the most important thing in his life.

Food journal—As the Daniel Plan recommends, he kept a journal of the food he was eating, down to the smallest thing, like a single hard candy or the milk in his morning coffee. This ritual helped him change what he was eating, because now he was conscious about it. It also provided positive reinforcement as he began to change his eating habits.

Water—He drank water throughout the day. Not only did that keep his body hydrated, but it also kept his belly full, making it a bit easier to avoid snacking.

Sleep—Before the Daniel Plan, Pastor Rick stayed up all night once or twice a week, a habit he now broke in order to get a good night's sleep every night. Research shows that sleep deprivation creates lower overall blood flow to the brain, leading to cravings and poor decisions about eating.

High-quality foods—He got rid of the junk food in his diet and focused on eating only high-quality, healthy foods. Pastor Rick urged his congregation to give up the three "white powders"—sugar, salt, and processed flour—as he had. He dropped grabbing a doughnut on the run in the morning, substituting a healthy breakfast instead, then eating smaller meals throughout the day and cutting out sugary drinks (soda, fruit juices, etc.). He dropped bread from his diet, as it immediately turns to sugar in the bloodstream. As a result, he no longer had the cravings he'd had before. Not least, he also ate more slowly, enjoying his food more, and he noticed when he felt full instead of overeating and stuffing himself without thinking.

Exercise—With the inspiration of the Daniel Plan and his community, he was able to start doing both strength training and cardiovascular exercise regularly.

Supplements—At the recommendation of the doctors who developed the Daniel Plan, Pastor Rick added some basic nutritional supplements—a multivitamin for overall health, omega-3 fatty acids for heart and brain health, and vitamin D for bone strength. (We aren't making this a general recommendation. You should follow your doctor's advice about supplements and educate yourself on your specific needs.)

Weekly support group—Noting that Daniel in the Old Testament had three friends, Pastor Rick has affirmed that the support of peers on the program made a huge difference in being able to stay on track with his commitments.

We invite you to adopt as much of the Daniel Plan as you can. It doesn't have to be in the context of any religious belief. The core issue here is how the mind and body complement each other. What you think affects how you feel. Modern medicine has validated this fact through decades of mind-body research, and now it's time to use the connection to prevent disease at the level of mind, which will then translate into how life energy flows through every cell of your body.

Ancient health systems are being revitalized around the world, bringing us knowledge that was either repressed or considered unscientific. Wisdom is their strength, beginning with the simplest piece of wisdom: Each of us has a unique nature. What may be the perfect remedy for one person could be ineffective for someone else. Unless you're already very sensitive, you'll notice your health issues only when they manifest on the material level of your Life Design. The energetic level is deeper and more subtle. Working on that level, it becomes possible to:

1. Identify health issues before they become physical problems.
2. Support the natural healing mechanisms in the body.
3. Address issues that may not respond to modern medical approaches.

The following ritual puts you in touch with the subtle imbalances that are the first sign of a disruption in the mind-body connection. These imbalances are often signaled by negative thoughts that need to be rechanneled in a healthier direction, since every thought, positive or negative, sends a message to your body.

RITUAL PRACTICE

Correcting Subtle Imbalances

We know that mind and body are connected, constantly exchanging messages and signals. On the mental level, this stream of messages takes the form of thoughts, sensations, and feelings. They can be read, however, as signals from your body, too. Being aware of these messages is a first-line defense against disease before symptoms appear, when your body is telling you it is out of balance.

Many people are not used to dealing with health issues on a level more subtle than the physical body. Yet modern medicine acknowledges that a high percentage of disease is psychosomatic (physical symptoms caused by mental or emotional disturbance). Doesn't it make sense to deal with such issues before they become physical problems?

Right this minute, and throughout the day, you are engaged in an internal dialogue that reaches all the way to your cells. When you repeatedly have self-destructive or self-sabotaging thoughts and feelings (projected from the mental and emotional level), they can ultimately manifest in your body as illness. You can dissolve the negative effects of such mental or emotional patterns using the following technique recommended by Master Stephen Co, leading practitioner and teacher of Pranic Healing:

> When you notice a thought or feeling arising repeatedly that causes you distress, put your attention between your eyebrows. Then repeat to yourself, "This thought (or emotion) is completely erased and disintegrated." Then bring to mind the feeling you would like to experience in place of what you have erased. Do this by remembering a time when you felt that emotion very strongly. Repeat this sequence several times, then go about your day.

If the negative thought or emotion comes up again, repeat the practice. Continue doing this whenever the thought or emotion arises, and you will discover it arising less and less until it no longer comes up at all.

Try it out this coming week. Just choose one thought or emotion that is disturbing for you and repeat this practice whenever it arises. See what happens.

BEAUTY RITUALS: DAWN'S STORY

Dawn Gallagher loved her summers in the country. Being one of eight kids, she never lacked for entertainment. Summer meant leaving the city behind, which was a relief. Back in Buffalo, life wasn't so rosy. Dawn's family lived in a rough part of the city. Because she was tall and lanky, all through middle school the boys would bully her. They told her how ugly she was, and many a time she ran away to cry in private.

Part of every summer was spent at her grandmother's. Dawn's grandmother was a beautiful Italian woman who would wrap her up in hugs and kisses when she came with her brothers and sisters. She also loved caring for her beauty, and the rituals that went with it. She held that if something came from the earth, it was meant to be used. Dawn learned how to make facial masks from bananas or avocados, yogurt and honey. Grandma would say, "Everything you need for beauty can be found in the earth, your cupboard, or your refrigerator."

RITUAL PRACTICE

Tahitian Mask

The mask we recommend takes its ingredients from the cupboard and the refrigerator, just as Dawn's grandmother advised. Women have been using such masks for centuries to brighten dull, lifeless skin. Have fun with this by putting on some soothing music, lighting a candle, and perfuming the room with incense. Set your intent to look and feel beautiful. Then follow the recipe and the guidelines that follow.

Tahitian Mask (for normal or oily skin)

Ylang-ylang is indigenous to the Maya Archipelago. Dawn noticed the women of Tahiti mixing ylang-ylang with their coconut oil and using it as an all-over body rub and in their hair.

1 teaspoon of honey
1 teaspoon of crushed oatmeal
½ cup of plain yogurt
1 teaspoon of Wheatena brand cereal
1 drop of geranium oil
1 drop of ylang-ylang oil

Warm the honey and add to the oatmeal, yogurt, and Wheatena. Add in the drops of essential oils and make a thick paste. Apply the mask to your face, then lie back and leave it on for 10 to 20 minutes.

(Adapted with permission from Dawn Gallagher at www.dawngallagher.com.)

By the time she was seventeen, Dawn's days of being bullied were behind her. It was parade day in Buffalo, and she was strolling the streets with her brother and sister. Unexpectedly, a man approached her wearing a camera around his neck. He introduced himself as Ron Keneske. "I work with some of the top modeling agencies in New York," he said, "and I think you really have the potential to be a very successful model. Are you interested?"

Dawn's brother Danny angrily rebuffed the stranger. "She's not interested. Now, get out of here." Clearly this was some creep trying to hit on her.

The man with the camera shrugged. "Take my card at least. If you change your mind, give me a call."

Dawn kept the card as a memento of the day a photographer thought she was pretty enough to be a model. Some time later she happened on an article in the *Buffalo News* about models who had been discovered in Buffalo. Her eyes widened when she read that Ron Keneske was responsible for discovering some of the world's top models, such as Beverly Johnson, Kim Alexis, and Linda Evangelista. "Oh, my God," she thought. "This guy is for real!"

Like any protective father, her dad was skeptical when she showed him the article. But with eight children at home, he wasn't in a position to send all of them to college. He agreed to phone on Dawn's behalf, and she got an appointment to have some photos made to be sent around to modeling agencies in New York.

Dawn could only imagine how modeling might affect her life. Fortunately, Ron was patient and gentle at her first shoot, showing her how to stand, how to hold her head, and other basics. Dawn felt stiff and awkward, but she did what he told her. Shy as she was, all the attention being paid to her was new and flattering. There were encouraging words at the end. "We got some great shots. I'll send them off to New York, and we'll see what they say."

Dawn was dumbstruck when she got a call from John Casablancas, head of Elite Model Management, one of the top fashion firms in Paris and New York, with branches worldwide. He sounded quite enthusiastic. "I've seen your shots, and I think you have the potential to be really big in the modeling world. I'd like to meet you."

In short order Casablancas flew to Buffalo to meet her and present a contract. Her parents took pains to ensure that their daughter would be cared for and protected when she took the leap to the big city at such a young age. When summer came, she left home and found herself in a very different world. The career of a budding supermodel had begun.

Today, Dawn has appeared on the covers of over 300 magazines, including *Vogue, Cosmopolitan, Harper's Bazaar,* and *Redbook.* It became a mission for her to give back to the millions of beauty-conscious readers who look at models as icons of beauty. They needed to gain a connection to beauty as an attainable state for themselves, not a faraway ideal. To offer guidance, Dawn wrote two books, *Naturally Beautiful* and *Nature's Beauty Secrets.* Here's one of her beauty rituals that we enjoy and endorse.

RITUAL PRACTICE

Dawn's Moisturizing Ritual

Ritual should enhance your life, and there's every reason why your rituals can be fun. Why not enjoy making yourself beautiful by turning the process into a ritual?

In her worldwide travels to fashion shoots, Dawn learned about a moisturizer that can be used following your application of the Tahitian mask.

Pampering Rose Moisturizer

You can find great sources for the essential oils in this recipe at Dawn's site, www.dawngallagher.com.

2 teaspoons of jojoba oil
3 teaspoons of sweet almond oil

3 drops of rose essential oil

I to 2 drops of jasmine or lavender essential oil

Mix the jojoba oil and sweet almond oil together as a base. Combine the essential oils together, and then add to the base oil. You can experiment with your own favorite essential oil(s), depending on your skin type. Remember, just a few drops goes a long way. Smooth the moisturizing oil all over your face, neck, and shoulders. (Make sure your hands are clean.)

Supermodels—as has often been pointed out—represent a body image that very few women can realistically attain. As a result, the girls who adore supermodels and envy their careers are set up for failure, or so they feel. Yet any woman can use beauty as a way to increase her self-esteem in addition to caring for her body. This begins by making beauty a part of a holistic approach to health—looking more beautiful can be a path to being healthier.

For the ancient Mesopotamians, attending to personal care and cleanliness was a ritual with religious overtones. Ritual bathing was almost universal throughout the ancient world. From a modern medical perspective, the skin is the body's largest organ; in the past few decades it has been discovered that skin secretes more hormones than any other organ. The enemies of health are also enemies of the complexion. Water and air pollution, harsh light, stress, smoking, poor diet, and lack of exercise all leave their mark on your skin. Its tone and color are also a barometer of emotions (as anyone knows who has turned red with embarrassment or pale with fright). When you care for it well, you glow, because the energetic level of your Life Design is shining through your skin.

Beauty rituals are for the purpose of nurturing yourself. By taking time and care over moisturizers, masks, and creams that nourish your skin, you reinforce the belief that you matter. In short, beauty rituals are part of the self-care we discussed earlier in the chapter on foundation rituals.

RITUAL PRACTICE

Seeing Your Beauty

You can turn the routine of putting on makeup and blow-drying your hair into self-care rituals by thinking about your purpose in doing these things. When your beauty routines become a conscious act of devotion for someone you love, for instance, it becomes a fulfilling ritual.

You can reinforce the purpose behind beauty by taking a moment to close your eyes and remind yourself of your intention for making yourself beautiful. "I am here to celebrate the feminine in every way. I want my inner beauty to shine, and I feel that beauty as I make myself beautiful on the outside as well."

But there's no need to feel solemn—for countless women, their intention with beauty is to have fun—and we're all for it. So at moments of happiness and enjoyment, say to yourself, "I am glowing with beauty. I radiate it from my own being."

These affirmations link inner and outer beauty in a way that improves your self-worth in everything you are and do.

Beauty is a topic aimed at women, but men need the same self-care as it applies to their skin. Shaving rituals have been part of many cultures for thousands of years. Coming-of-age ceremonies were attached to a teenage boy beginning to shave. Now most men just whisk an electric shaver or a disposable plastic razor across their stubble as quickly as possible. No ritual could be made more empty than this, and millions of men look upon shaving as a necessary nuisance. But as long as you're doing it, take time to look at your skin in terms of health. A man's physical presence may not be associated so much with glowing skin as a woman's, but his well-being is reflected in healthy skin nonetheless. Look in the mirror and meet the person you see there. Affirm to yourself that you are proud of him and want to be the best man you can be.

RITUAL PRACTICE

The Shaving Ritual

If it appeals to you, you can turn shaving into a more elaborate ritual, the kind that men followed for centuries before electric and disposable razors came along. Men of an earlier generation enjoyed the relaxing ministrations of a barber. We're unlikely to return to the days when the barbershop was the center of male activity every morning, a place to socialize and make deals, but you can re-create the same ritual at home and get the same pleasure.

Begin by getting the proper shaving materials. You'll need a pre-shave gel, oil, or cream, along with a cake of shaving soap, and a quality badger hair brush (or, for the ethically minded, a good synthetic brush like Jack Black's award-winning synthetic Pure Performance Shave Brush). For removing whiskers, tradition calls for a well-balanced double-edged razor, the kind that holds razor blades. For the less committed, a high-quality multiblade disposable razor like the Gillette Fusion will do. Finally, have a non-alcohol-based aftershave on hand. Steam a wet face cloth for a minute in the microwave or just run it under very hot water for a few seconds then place it in a covered bowl for cleaning your face of shaving soap.

Now that you have everything you need to make everyday shaving a special experience, soak your brush in hot water in the sink while you take a shower. The hot water will open your pores and soften the bristles in your beard. After splashing warm water on your face, apply your pre-shave to soften up your beard. Next, take your brush out of the water where it's been soaking, shake out the excess water, then dip the brush into your shaving soap. A cake of good-quality soap will last a long time. If you use cream instead, lather it onto your face with your brush.

Using up-and-down motions, distribute the soap evenly, repeating the motions until you have an opaque lather covering your beard. Managing a traditional double-edged razor takes a little practice. The main thing is to use a *very light touch*. Don't bear down or you'll risk cutting yourself; just persevere, and you'll end up with the smoothest, softest face your woman has ever kissed.

After removing the last flecks of lather with your steamed hand cloth, finish off your ritual with a splash of aftershave. Then, go find someone you love, gently rub your face against hers, and be prepared for the oohs and aahs!

For both sexes, lasting beauty comes from within, and how you feel about yourself is ultimately what is most important. In a woman, a beautiful face is not created but only enhanced by putting on makeup. When a man treats himself to a great shave, he honors his manhood and himself. Self-care deserves to be personal, psychological, and even spiritual. A glowing complexion is, more than anything else, a reflection of radiant health, vitality, and happiness as the life force radiating from the transcendent center of your Life Design is expressed on the level of your material form.

We've been building a case for how to answer a question that touches everyone's life: What does it mean to be healthy? The average person thinks that being healthy means having no symptoms of disease. In traditional healing systems, the definition is much fuller. In Islam, the Quran describes health as:

> . . . a state of complete physical, mental, spiritual, and social well-being, which must be safeguarded not only through the maintenance of a health-preserving regimen at the personal/individual level, but also through the establishment of a health-protective and -promoting family system and a health-protective and -promoting social system.

These words could have come from the modern wellness movement. Wellness becomes even more powerful when it rests upon a foundation of wisdom. The principle of prevention has existed for our entire lifetime, yet without wisdom, people shrug off the risks and don't follow the best advice. Wellness requires you to value yourself enough to take action. For us, the framework of rituals is the best motivator for wellness, because an ingrained ritual carries the force of habit—your routine contains all the small things that protect your body without having to think about it every day. If you'd like support in designing health rituals for your life, we've gathered a collection of both ancient and modern health rituals at www.thehiddenriches.com/health.

If you wanted a protective shield to keep stress and disease at bay, you already possess it. It's your consciousness. With conscious intent you can envelop your body in rituals for self-care, vitality, beauty, and perfect weight. With foundation rituals you give your body the balance and regularity it craves. With relationship rituals you place your body in a loving, supportive atmosphere. With spiritual rituals you give your body the context of true meaning, something worth living for—a vision of never-ending personal growth. Since all these layers are contained in your Life Design, we consider it the perfect guide to health—nothing that makes you unique has been left out.

THE ART OF CREATING
WEALTH THROUGH RITUAL

*Pretend that every single person you meet has a sign
around their neck that says, "Make me feel important." Not
only will you succeed in sales, you will succeed in life.*

—MARY KAY ASH

There has never been a time when humans didn't enjoy prosperity or devise elaborate rituals to create it. Today, when modern capitalism is so successful in creating wealth globally, do rituals still have a meaningful role to play? Will they help you create more abundance in your life? Yes, although we don't always use the term "ritual" for the habits, routines, and ways of thinking that characterize those who travel a steady path to wealth and success. But they are aligned with their Life Design, at least in the area of money.

Dr. Stephen R. Covey created a major bestseller when he outlined what he called "the seven habits of highly effective people." One focus of these habits was efficient management of time and energy, as we discussed in the first chapter, "A Vision of Fulfillment." But there's more to achieving success than habits; deeper principles of the mind apply. Our method is to take the guesswork out of methods for success and make unconscious habits and routines conscious and purposeful. We will identify the core elements of your Life Design as related to wealth. For each element, we've created rituals that will amplify success in your own life. First, let's see what the path to uncovering someone's Life Design looks like.

Twenty-seven years old, three kids, and no husband anymore. "I felt like a complete and total failure," Mary remembers.

It was 1945; her husband of eleven years and the father of her three children had returned from the war and suddenly asked for a divorce. Mary needed a job that would give her flexibility to be with her kids yet provide enough income with no man in the house. Her mind went back to an incident before the war. A young woman had appeared at Mary's door selling encyclopedias. Perhaps sensing the drive in this young housewife, the woman told Mary she could have a free set if she sold ten sets to others. With no idea that selling ten sets of encyclopedias was the company's three-month quota for its sales force, Mary sold the sets in a day and a half.

At a time when few women worked outside the home, Mary chose direct sales based on demonstrating home products at "parties" that could be hosted by a housewife. From the start Mary thrived. She loved the social interaction and meeting new people. She was in her element. Seven years later a new outfit, World Gift Company, lured her away. She was promoted to national training director, extended the company's reach to forty-three states, and was then appointed to the board of directors. Mary's rise was impressive.

All the pieces seemed to be coming together when she met and then married George Hallenbeck in 1960. But by 1963 work had become a source of constant frustration. "I was always being told, 'Oh, Mary, you're thinking like a woman.' And inevitably no matter how hard I tried, or how well I did my job, I still found myself reaching the golden door only to find it marked, Men Only."

When she returned from a business trip to discover that her male assistant had been promoted to be her boss at double her salary, it was the last straw. She quit the next day. Her children were now grown and leading their own lives. The two roles that had defined her for almost twenty-seven years, mother and sales executive, were abruptly gone. "I've never spent a more miserable time. I just felt my life was over. My house was across the street from a mortuary, and I almost called them." She was at a crossroads and couldn't see the enormous success that lay ahead. Mary was about to become known to the public as the founder of Mary Kay Cosmetics.

When life is tough, it's no fun for anyone. The wealthy and successful, like everyone else, have faced crises of their own. What distinguishes them is resilience. They navigate through a crisis without being defeated by it. If there is one common characteristic among the self-made wealthy, it is an unwavering attention to the object of their passions, combined with an ongoing commitment to taking action. When they get knocked down, they find the motivation to pick themselves up and start focusing on what's working in their lives rather than what isn't. You can use rituals to cope with a crisis by using them to return to the core of your life—from your center, it becomes easier to ride the waves.

Money is often a focus for discomfort because our minds have been so programmed to believe money brings happiness and the lack of it is a sign of failure and personal weakness. Yet more money means more responsibility, the requirements of managing it, along with all the worry that it brings. Also, having more money often throws into high relief the psychological issues a person has around money. You can wake up at night with anxiety over getting down to your last hundred dollars or your last million. The issues are inside you, not inside your bank account. For someone who has made peace with having—or not having—wealth, money can serve a higher purpose, as a measuring stick for how much service they can offer to others. There are rituals for becoming the best at whatever you're passionate about, and then financial success is a by-product.

Mary Kay Ash, as she was now known, had a natural talent for direct sales, yet what made her unique was her passion for helping women faced with the same barriers she had faced. She built a company based on values that women could appreciate, even if few men could. At the height of her success she would send out thousands of personally addressed birthday cards to her "consultants" and call when she heard about a sickness in the family. For Mary Kay, her mission wasn't about making lots of money. "I was never interested in the dollars-and-cents part of business. My interest was in offering women opportunities that didn't exist anywhere else."

So how do you get from A to B, from doing work that is good enough, brings home the bacon, and provides a bit of security, to doing work that brings real fulfillment and calls upon the best you can be?

In the first chapter we discussed the importance of rituals for managing time and energy. We said that ultimately all rituals are about managing your mind in order to tap into its hidden potential. Let's go deeper into that area, since passion is only the first step in uncovering your Life Design. Once it is uncovered, your Life Design does more than express your passion.

It gives you the strength to overcome obstacles.

It keeps a steady flow of inspiration coming your way.

It provides a sense of freshness and renewal.

It opens your eyes so that you can see ahead before crises arise.

When you are faced with a new challenge along your journey, it offers creative solutions.

These aren't incidental as a person realizes their potential. They are essential. People like Mary Kay Ash, who seemed to have discovered her destiny in an exceptional way, didn't make up their Life Design. No one handed them—or will hand you—a blueprint that can be followed by simply studying the plans and carrying them out. Part of the mystery of life is that you are required to uncover your unique Life Design for yourself.

Your Life Design is a pattern of the ideal life, yet it is full of challenge, change, and opportunity, which means that you need to remain alert, open, and willing to enter the unknown every step of the way. Beneath the chaotic surface, where events seem random and good fortune appears to come only to the select few, everyone has an ideal life waiting for them.

However, your brain doesn't automatically know that this is true. Trained to treat life as a series of ups and downs without rhyme or reason, your brain largely works in survival mode. It is on the lookout for the next danger. It tries to disguise fear and weakness from others. It works overtime to make tomorrow as predictable as yesterday. Your Life Design holds the key to a more fulfilling approach. The more you align with it, as you are learning to in this book, the more your brain will start looking for ways to maximize the positive rather than the negative. That's where real transformation comes from.

True passion is inspirational and leads to making decisions that work toward carrying out your intentions. Passing infatuations, on the other hand, tend to fizzle out. The brightest ideas often don't lead to the necessary steps for turning them into reality, because there needs to be more depth of commitment, which is what passion supplies.

Mary Kay's story illustrates the difference that real passion makes. In an attempt to get beyond her depression over quitting her

job, she started writing down things she had done well and obstacles she had overcome. As she made her list, she realized how much
she had learned in twenty-five years of sales. Maybe she could write
a management book that would help other women. As she began
to outline the book, she began thinking about what characteristics
would define a "dream company." The more she thought about it,
the more she asked herself why she wanted to just write about a
dream company. Why not create one? Suddenly she started to get
excited.

Hers would be a direct sales company, because that's where her
skill and talent lay. It had to work for women, including housewives
and mothers tied to the home. Employees needed to be able to work
their own hours, whether they were full- or part-time. The most
crucial decision, Mary Kay realized, was what line of products to
offer, something her consultants, as she called them, could believe
in and recommend without reservation. To ensure ongoing profit-
ability, the product had to be something that got used up, leading to
regular reorders.

As she and her husband, George, were talking through these
points, Mary Kay reached an "Aha!" moment. Years earlier, she'd
given a sales demonstration at the end of which the hostess started
selling her own private-label skin cream to the participants. Noticing what incredible skin her hostess had, Mary Kay picked up some
cream for herself. After using the product for more than a decade,
she was in love with it and never failed to place a reorder. The way
ahead was now clear. She and George scraped together $5,000 and
bought the formula from the inventor's heirs. They furnished an office in downtown Dallas and contracted with a local manufacturer
to make a line of skin-care products based on the cream she'd been
using all those years.

Mary Kay worked on recruiting sales reps while her husband

focused on the legal and financial side of the business. She had nine of her friends lined up to sell their products, and in about a month they would be ready to open for business. Everything was coming together.

And then George died. It came as a huge blow, but like many entrepreneurs before her, Mary Kay's passion wouldn't allow her to give up on her dream in the face of adversity. She talked with her young son, twenty-year-old Richard Rogers.

"I worshipped the ground she walked on," Richard says, and so when his mother asked for his help and support, he gave up his job selling insurance to jump in and help start her new company, Beauty by Mary Kay.

They both knew that she was going up against a giant in direct sales, the seventy-seven-year-old Avon brand. Every woman in America knew about the Avon lady who rang the doorbell in their television commercials. But Mary Kay was taking a different tack. Rather than Avon's approach of door-to-door sales, she turned the selling process into an enjoyable and effective ritual. She trained her consultants to identify hostesses for in-home parties. These parties were carefully scripted to build on the natural desire of women to connect and socialize. They became a huge and instantaneous hit.

Mary Kay Cosmetics overcame the odds. Starting with good products, sound marketing, and a smart business plan, the company grew quickly. Her attention to celebrating her consultants' success was a central part of her strategy. The company institutionalized rituals that became part of its uniqueness. For example, Mary Kay hit upon handing out diamond-encrusted bumblebees at each annual meeting as a metaphor for what she and the women she'd inspired were doing: "Aerodynamically, bumblebees shouldn't be able to fly, but the bumblebee doesn't know that, so it goes on flying anyway." Giving away the bees and, for the top producers, a pink Cadillac was an annual ritual at company gatherings that set Mary Kay Cosmetics apart and gave consultants a sense of pride in being self-sufficient women. Today, the company has more than $2.5 billion a year in sales and more than 1.5 million consultants worldwide.

Even when you're following your passions and doing what brings you joy, there will be tough times. The rituals you use to respond to these times can make all the difference in your success. You can build up the inner resources that Mary Kay displayed. She had her own combination of natural gifts and challenges, as you do. She created rituals in her company that reflected her own passions as they expressed themselves through her Life Design. Like Mary Kay, rituals can give you, and those around you, a foundation for strength, purpose, and motivation.

HOW RITUAL FITS INTO SUCCESS

There has been a growing recognition in management literature of the importance of rites and rituals in creating successful companies:

"Without expressive events, any [corporate] culture will die. In the absence of ceremony or ritual, important values have no impact." —*Corporate Cultures: The Rites and Rituals of Corporate Life* by Terrence E. Deal and Allan A. Kennedy

"What distinguishes the culture of 'excellent' corporations is their conscious use of 'rites and rituals' to give their employees a sense of belonging and make their work seem more meaningful." —*The Chinese Transformation of Corporate Culture* by Colin Hawes

"Great performers, whether they are athletes, or fighter pilots, surgeons or Special Forces soldiers, FBI agents or CEOs, all rely on positive rituals to manage their energy and achieve their goals." —*The Power of Full Engagement* by Jim Loehr and Tony Schwartz

Consciously or unconsciously, people like Mary Kay develop rituals that support them no matter what their external situation or circumstances. Here are some of the elements that appear to be at the core of what makes people financially successful, which means these are things that allow your Life Design to unfold naturally. In parentheses we've noted how each of these relates to the five levels of your inner life we've discussed before:

Passion (the Level of Bliss)
Certainty of Success (the Level of Knowingness)
Vision (the Level of Mind)
Embracing Change (the Level of the Energetic)
Measuring the Results (the Level of the Material Form)

Let's talk a little more about each of these and give you rituals to develop each of these qualities.

Passion—the Level of Bliss

The reason successful people so often say "Follow your passion" is that your passions bring joy, meaning, and a feeling of purpose—ultimately you will discover your Life Design along the path of joy. Someone else may have made a bundle in real estate, stock investments, or selling on eBay, but if those life paths don't bring you joy, they won't bring you sustainable wealth or fulfillment. For Mary Kay, her talent for connecting with people made direct sales a natural fit. Your natural fit depends on something you truly love. A burning desire to do great things is tied to your destiny. That desire is actually built into your Life Design.

RITUAL PRACTICE

The Passion Test

The first ritual to establish in your life if you want to create more wealth is the practice of regularly identifying those things that matter most to you, your passions. This is not a onetime exercise; for us, it's a regular ritual we repeat every four to six months. Once you're clear on your top passions, then choose in favor of them consistently and you will begin living the injunction Steve Jobs gave in 2005, when he delivered the commencement address at Stanford:

> Your work is going to fill a large part of your life, and the only way to be truly satisfied is to do what you believe is great work. And the only way to do great work is to love what you do. If you haven't found it yet, keep looking. Don't settle. As with all matters of the heart, you'll know when you find it. And, like any great relationship, it just gets better and better as the years roll on. So keep looking until you find it. Don't settle.

There's a reason the Passion Test has become the number one tool used worldwide to discover your passions and connect with your life purpose. It's based on the principle that when you know the five things that matter most to you in your life, then begin to consistently make decisions that help you be more connected to those things, you can't help but live a passionate, turned-on life.

The first step is to find out where you stand in living your passions right now. Then you can go through the Passion Test process to identify your passions and create a vision for your life. To get started with your free Passion Profile Assessment, go to www.thepassiontest.com.

Certainty of Success—the Level of Knowingness

Those who have earned their own fortunes have the ability to dream big and to maintain an unshakable sense that their dreams can be achieved. Warren Buffett was once quoted as saying: "I always knew I would be rich. I don't think I ever doubted it for a minute."

If you don't already have this "inner knowingness," rituals can help you develop it. Knowingness is always there, but it's often sidetracked by doubt, insecurity, and other sabotaging beliefs. It begins with how you view being rich. Do you believe that "money is the root of all evil" or that "the rich get richer and the poor get poorer"? If so, why would you ever choose to be rich? Then you'd be one of the greedy, selfish, bad guys. Until and unless you view your wealth as a gift—for yourself, those around you, and for the world—you are unlikely to ever fully open the doors to abundance.

The good news is you don't have to try to change those patterns and beliefs, you just have to stop feeding them. The way you do that is by beginning to feed new ways of thinking that will support what you choose to create in the world.

RITUAL PRACTICE

Transforming Your Beliefs About Money

Having constructive beliefs around money and wealth is important on the way to achieving wealth. Many people are held back by negative beliefs. They unconsciously feel that they don't deserve to be rich. They believe that money is somehow tainted. They associate it with greed and corruption. Any of these negative beliefs can slow you down or even throw you off track to winning real financial success.

Below we've adapted the rituals that work for achieving the ideal relationship, which makes sense once you realize that lack of money isn't really the problem. It's your relationship with it that creates challenges. If you want to be wealthy, it's time to invite it into your life, just as you would invite your perfect romantic partner.

1. Write out your feelings and beliefs about money, including any stereotypes about greedy Scrooges and ruthless millionaires. Get personal—write down how you felt about losing money, not having enough, or feeling insecure about your personal finances. Looking ahead, are you afraid you won't have enough money in the future? Are your present expenses and debts weighing you down? Be thorough. Once you have your list, tear it into tiny pieces and let the wind carry all those old, stale concepts away.

2. Find a beach or other location where you will be completely alone. Shout into the air all the "gunk" related

to money that you're now ready to release. To bring up these feelings, see yourself in past situations where you felt helpless, ashamed, or fearful about money, those times when money worries made you feel trapped.

3. Sit with a friend and describe the heartfelt desires and intentions you have for your life. Talk about how you will use the money you are now ready to accept. How will you use it to improve both your own life and the lives of others? Have the intention to remove all traces of your past dysfunctional relationship with money. Your new path should include a plan to pay off any debt you've accumulated (the Jar Ritual later in this chapter is really helpful for this).

4. Begin making room in your life for the money that is not yet here, but that you are beginning to feel could soon show up. With a ledger or financial software, create separate accounts for the different parts of your life that you'll use your money for: donations, large purchases (house, car, appliances, etc.), education, financial freedom (investments), and fun, in addition to the account for your necessities.

5. Receive a consultation in feng shui (or an even older tradition for creating optimal energy flow in your house, India's Sthapatya Veda, also known as *vastu shastra*). Arrange your space so that it will support the attraction of more money into your life. If you can, do the same with your work space.

6. Get yourself out of the house. Find friends you enjoy who are good with money. Hang out with them, do things for them, find ways you can support them so that

they will be happy to have you around. There's truth to the adage "You become like those with whom you spend time."

7. Like the self-made British billionaire Richard Branson, make a point to carry a notebook or a tablet computer with you all the time. When a stroke of genius hits you, record it immediately for follow-up later. Putting down a record also helps to imprint your idea and fix your intention before it drifts away.

8. Another tip from Branson: Set aside specific times in your week for learning about the areas you love and are passionate about. Mark the time on your calendar and make it a priority, even if other appointments cause a potential conflict. This is a way of honoring the time you invest in your personal joy and enrichment. Visualize your path to success.

Dan Jansen was a speed-skating sprinter who was favored to win gold at the 1988 Winter Olympics in Calgary when his sister died of leukemia just before the final race. He ended up taking a spill, and the picture of him sitting on the ice with his head in his hands became an enduring image of abject despair.

When he returned to training, a key element was taking time to sit in a special chair in a designated room surrounded by the medals, trophies, and photos representing everything he had achieved so far. There were also images and symbols of what he wanted to achieve in the future. Jansen spent a lot of time in this room visualizing his upcoming races, picturing any unexpected situations, and mentally rehearsing how he would handle them.

In 1994 at the Winter Games in Lillehammer, Norway, he

went on to win gold in the 1,000-meter race in world record time. Interestingly, he had always been favored to win the 500 and had never liked the 1,000-meter race. But through his rituals, he lost his aversion to the longer distance. In the end, it was the race he won. This is why in *The Passion Test* we say to stay open to what is appearing in your life, because the fulfillment of your passions may not come in the exact way you think it will.

Vision—the Level of Mind

A big vision inspires people. It provides a road map for where to put your attention and a "why" for all the hard work you're doing. Friedrich Nietzsche said, "He who has a why to live for can bear almost any how." One of the things that will help you keep going when things get tough is what Stephen Covey describes as beginning with the end in mind. A good example would be when FedEx was founded. Key to its success was the vision that a company aiming to compete with the U.S. Post Office in package delivery had to have a nationally connected air fleet, a rapid procedure for routing packages, a central hub, and outreach to every city and town in America. Unless the end point was taken into account, FedEx could not have existed.

Motivation calls upon two things that aren't easy to match: where you are today and where you will be at the end of the process. That's why we recommend an annual ritual of writing out or recording your "100th birthday speech."

RITUAL PRACTICE

Your 100th Birthday Speech

Imagine you're at your 100th birthday party, surrounded by the people you love. Someone dear to you is giving a speech outlining all of the contributions you've made in your long life and the legacy you've left for others. What would they say? Imagine an ideal account of your life and put it into words.

Once you've clarified what the end result will look like, take the current project that's in front of you and create a five-year plan with as much detail as you are able (getting help with this phase is a really good idea because few people can think of all possible outcomes, including what could go wrong). Update your 100th birthday speech and your five-year plan each year (or more often if your results are significantly different from your plan). By continually matching the ideal with the actual, you are putting your vision into practice.

Here are a few helpful principles:

Reality is always right, but it leaves room so that you can be right, too.

Visions must change as circumstances change.

Obstacles are signposts, pointing you to what needs more work.

Inspiration is always better than motivation, because motivation always has a shelf life before it expires. Sometimes the shelf life is very short.

Hard work and determination need reward and celebration. Without them, they become dry and without joy.

RITUAL PRACTICE

Reward Your Vision

One of the most important things you can do along your path to financial abundance is to set down well-defined incentives and rewards, both for yourself and your team. Set financial targets on a monthly, quarterly, and annual basis. Itemize separate categories for your total revenue, net income, and savings.

Now establish rewards for each target you achieve. Your annual targets should have the biggest rewards, naturally, but your monthly rewards should be worth achieving, too. Give yourself the most significant rewards for the targets that are the hardest to achieve. When rewarding others, imagination counts. Using her own love of competition as a marker, Mary Kay created distinctive rewards for her top producers. The Cadillacs that were painted pink to match the Mary Kay cosmetic line and diamond bumblebees became novel symbols incorporated into corporate rituals that reinforced that this was a company designed to be more family than corporate.

At the beginning of each month, create a ritual celebration. You might do it on the first Saturday of every month. Review your targets for the previous month, then award prizes for success. Give yourself a treat you wouldn't normally indulge in, such as a massage treatment or a ticket to an NBA basketball game.

The best way to benefit from the Ritual of Reward is to find a buddy or, even better, a group of friends who will join in it with you. Whether you choose to share your financial numbers with each other or not, you can hold each other accountable for checking the balance books every month and treating each other as you hit your targets. This way, your vision is becoming tangible step by step, with increasing confidence and pride.

Embracing Change—the Level of the Energetic

The only constant in life is change. Events unfold differently from what we expect, and those who have amassed great wealth and kept it were able to deal with unpredictability. Their response to change moved them forward, while for most people, unexpected events can be paralyzing. Rest assured, every rise to success met with shocks and surprises along the way. Even potentially devastating obstacles can become part of your path. It all depends on whether you see them as weaknesses or not. Richard Branson, Charles Schwab, Henry Ford, Cher, Tom Cruise, and Whoopi Goldberg were all dyslexic, yet it didn't stop them from rising to the top of their fields.

Meeting with obstacles is inevitable. They aren't a sign that you aren't supposed to be successful. They are there to help you determine how committed you are to your vision. When obstacles can't stop you, then they're part of your Life Design. The beauty of knowing that you have a hidden pattern waiting to be uncovered is that you can look upon obstacles as clues in a scavenger hunt. The best scavenger hunts are messy—half the fun is finding the next clue under a slimy rock or buried in mud. Slime and mud aren't appealing on their own, but if you are certain that a prize awaits at the end of the hunt, they become fun—part of the pleasure of reaching your goal is to look back on the trials it took to get there.

The key along the path is your ability to discover how each obstacle and challenge serve you in fulfilling your vision. To help, we've created a Discover the Gift ritual, which you can use as a powerful tool to change the way you respond to change and the unexpected turns that life takes.

RITUAL PRACTICE

Discover the Gift

Every moment in your life is filled with gifts. However, when something bad happens, it's hard to find the gift within the apparent disaster. Knowing that your greatest achievements may actually come on the heels of your greatest catastrophes, start practicing the Discover the Gift ritual before crisis strikes.

Begin with gratitude. Spend ten minutes at the end of each day writing down five to ten things you're grateful for from that day and *why* you're grateful for each. By asking why, you'll go to a deeper level, and your gratitude will have stronger emotional content. Strong emotional content is the missing ingredient that makes ritual effective rather than empty.

Once you've established gratitude as a ritual in your life, you're ready to discover the gift. As you write down the things you're grateful for, add one or two things that were really challenging from that day. Take a moment to think about the benefit that came with the challenge. How did it help you see something from a different perspective or to gain more clarity about what you're doing? Did you handle a difficult person better, or a difficult situation? Were you more in control? Did you find an unexpected solution to a problem?

These are the gifts that come wrapped up with obstacles and

resistance. They don't emerge unless you look for them and pay attention—otherwise, a bad day is just a bad day. Once you take satisfaction in the silver lining, the dark cloud goes away.

As you record the gifts that come with even the most challenging parts of your life, you'll notice how your perspective changes. There's no longer anything to fear about meeting obstacles on your path, because you know there will always be a gift waiting for you.

Measuring the Results—the Level of the Material Form

Here's where the "rubber meets the road." Wealthy people use money as a measuring stick for their success in providing value. Beyond the raw numbers, making a profit in business points to happy customers, job security for workers, and promotion for managers. At any rung of income, when you receive money, whether as a salary from an employer or as purchases from customers, it's an indication that you're providing something that others believe is valuable.

Sustainable wealth happens when the value you are giving is more than the value people are paying. Whether it's the free half tube of toothpaste or the extra care to build a totally reliable automobile or performing a job exceptionally well, added value is the secret. This is where that old adage "Underpromise and overdeliver" comes into play. When what's delivered is greater than what was promised, people will come back again and again. Word of mouth, whether from customers or co-workers, will promote you as no amount of glossy advertising can, and your income will continue to grow.

Those who have created their own wealth closely monitor their financial results, even if those results are disappointing. Objective measurements tell you:

1. If you're providing something others see as valuable.
2. How effectively you're serving the needs of others.
3. What you need to do to be even more effective.

The common purpose we all share, the built-in element in every Life Design, is to be of service to the people around us. This solves the dilemma of how much money to keep and how much to give away, how much is selfish and how much is altruistic. The two aren't opposites. They meet at the level of value. When real value and perceived value are aligned, you are serving the needs of others. At the same time, this alignment is the key to creating personal wealth for yourself.

Your value is intrinsic to you. It is embedded in your passions (the things you love and care about most), your talents (the things you do well naturally), and your skills (the things you've learned to do well). When you combine these three to fulfill the needs of others, you have the basis for a comfortable, fulfilled life. Measuring your results allows you to see how well you are doing in meeting the needs of others.

But if you want to change your present financial situation, measuring your results is not enough. You also need to take action based on those results. Adapt or change your strategy if you're not getting the outcome you want. Equally important is how you use the money you make. If your desire is to create wealth, you may need to change some old patterns from the past.

At this point we've connected the flow of money from its subtle origin to its final material expression. Your Life Design embraces all five levels.

MICHELLE'S STORY

Stories about self-made millionaires are inspiring, but what makes the difference between someone who parlays a few thousand dollars into a fortune and someone else who squanders a few thousand on a junket to Las Vegas? One of the ways to get started is by using a simple ritual to amplify your present finances, as Michelle did—it pays off in big dividends very quickly.

Michelle grew up in a comfortable middle-class family, but she didn't understand her parents. Her mom constantly clipped coupons; her dad hated to part with a penny. Why did they always skimp? They were frugal to the point of being cheap. It didn't make sense, and when Michelle grew up she made a point of buying the things she wanted. That was all well and good, except that over and over again, she found herself short of cash. She ran up her credit cards, then asked her parents for a loan to tide her over. When her cards maxed out, the debt to her parents had risen to $26,000, and she was teetering on the edge of bankruptcy. Michelle decided to attend one of T. Harv Eker's financial seminars. She knew she needed some strong guidance.

Eker introduced her to the Jar Ritual. This simple practice involves dividing one's income into six categories, or jars:

1. Necessities—money for rent, car payments, insurance, food, and other basic living expenses. Eker suggested setting a goal of limiting necessities to 50 percent of total income.
2. Donations—money to support charitable causes.
3. Large purchases—money to buy a new car, house, washing machine, computer, or other big expenses so you don't have to borrow to buy these things.

4. Education—money to expand your ability to be effective and successful.

5. Financial freedom account—money for investments to increase your wealth.

6. Fun—money to make the rest of it worthwhile.

But Michelle's problem was that she had no extra money. How was she going to put money into all these jars? Realizing the purpose of the Jar Ritual was to create the habit of being conscious about how she used her money, she started with a dollar. She put ten cents into each of the first five jars and fifty cents into her Necessities jar. She did this month after month, setting aside a dollar to divide between her jars. After a while she realized she wasn't going to build her wealth very much with a dollar a month, so she decided to double the amount she put in the jars. The next month she put in two dollars—a minuscule increase, but it represented progress.

And so it went, from two dollars to four, then eight. The ritual had her hooked, and eventually she was dividing up over two thousand dollars, at which point Michelle opened six bank accounts. They replaced the jars in her kitchen but served the same purpose of apportioning her money every month. She says that the Jar Ritual not only helped her start putting money aside for the things she needed and wanted, but also forced her to become more creative and to focus on increasing how much she was actually earning. Living within limits was impossible when her ideal was just to spend as she pleased. Thanks to the Jar Ritual, living within limits became a source of ingenuity and pride. She was especially proud to pay down her debts from the funds in her financial freedom account.

Here's an example of how a single ritual pulled someone back from the edge of bankruptcy. Within two years Michelle had paid off her entire debt, including the $26,000 she had borrowed from her "stingy" parents. No freedom tasted sweeter to her than financial freedom once she attained it, all from her own efforts. Beyond escaping debt, she attained more freedom when she amassed enough in that jar to take her first step into buying real estate. From one property, she bought another, and in time she owned almost a dozen rental properties. The old Michelle would have run wild with so much cash flow, but the new Michelle kept up the Jar Ritual, rigorously dividing up the money into six compartments.

Today Michelle is financially free. She travels the world, does what she wants, and follows her passion, which in her case means helping financially strapped people who find themselves in the same position where she began.

RITUAL PRACTICE

The Jar Ritual

Let's recap this powerful and effective way to change how you deal with the income and outlay of your money. The mind doesn't deal well with open-ended situations, much preferring to know in advance how to make decisions. It might seem that throwing money around is liberating; almost all the time, however, it's simply chaotic. Money is associated with all three things that need to be well organized in your life: time, energy, and thought. It is also associated with the pitfalls that exist in these areas: squandering your time, wasting your energy, and falling prey to compulsive thinking. (Someone who is addicted to shopping is acting out compulsive thinking, while at the other extreme, hoarders and penny-pinchers are being compulsive about spending as little as possible.)

Acquire six large jars and label them as Michelle did:

1. Necessities
2. Large Purchases
3. Donations
4. Education
5. Financial Freedom
6. Fun

Every time you get paid, decide on an amount you will use for the Jar Ritual. Divide this amount among the six jars. Put 50 percent into the Necessities jar and apportion the rest between the other five. When the amounts become too big to easily store in jars, open six bank accounts. But keep your jars and put your end-of-the-month bank statement for each account into them, along with deposit slips.

Tithing—Part of the Jar Ritual is setting aside funds for donations. It's one of the oldest rituals on earth—giving a portion of what you earn to support something greater than yourself. As our friend Robert Allen, author of the number one *New York Times* bestsellers *Creating Wealth* and *Nothing Down,* wrote about early billionaires from the Gilded Age such as John D. Rockefeller Jr.: "Many . . . looked upon their money as a sort of spiritual stewardship. Most of them believed that God gave them the money. If every dollar they received was a gift from God, they were glad to pay back 10 percent of it. (If I gave you a dollar, would you give me back ten cents?)"

If you're not comfortable with donating 10 percent of your

income, begin with 1 percent and gradually increase the amount. That way, by the end of your life, maybe you'll be like Warren Buffett and be able to give away 99 percent!

By the way, Chris has taught his six-year-old daughter, Sophie, to use the Jar Ritual, and you may want to try it with your own children. He has created a simple written agreement with Sophie outlining tasks she has agreed to do to support the family and the compensation she receives each week for performing these tasks. Then every week they sit together, she puts 50 percent of her money in her Necessities jar, and then divides the rest among the others. Each jar has an accounting sheet that has the date, who the money came from, the amount deposited in the jar or taken out, and the balance in the jar. Sophie is learning not only how to manage money, but also how to write numbers and letters and to add and subtract, all through this simple Jar Ritual.

Probably you began reading this chapter wondering how money could be influenced and encouraged through rituals. Now we hope you see how valuable it is to link the two. But there's much more to explore in this area. There is an abundance of knowledge from ancient cultures throughout the world about rituals for creating prosperity. We've gathered some of the most interesting and fun ones at www.thehiddenriches.com/wealth.

CEREMONIAL RITUALS
AND THE SEASONS OF LIFE

Each beautiful thing, a flower, the song of a bird,
Awakens in our soul the memory of our origin.
Learn how to listen to the voice of beautiful things,
To make us understand the voice of our soul.

—THE MEVLEVI DERVISHES

I t's time to expand our understanding of rituals dramatically in scope and scale. There's a vast new territory to explore. In the past, whole societies and cultures determined their destiny through religious and mythic ceremonies. All of nature was embraced, and the most primal forces of the mind were harnessed. Every ancient culture performed such rituals, but in modern society they have largely been lost. Now it's time to learn how to regain the feelings of connection, peace, and wholeness that were lost with them.

To help understand the full power of rituals, we can separate them into two categories: the simple everyday rituals (the kinds we've been discussing so far) and the more elaborate ceremonial rituals. Everyday rituals blend into your current routines and habits. Ceremonial rituals are more formal and for modern people are generally associated with special life events such as weddings or baptisms or graduations.

Ritual ceremonies permeate every religion, and these were preceded by even more ancient ones aimed at stirring the forces of nature—such as the fertility rituals of spring, meant to appease the gods and entice them to bring rain and an abundance of crops. Today most people look back on such performances as superstitious; in a generous mood, one might consider them cultural artifacts or naive religion. We think something much deeper was going on.

Ceremonial rituals awaken the sacred. They create sacred spaces. They mark the sacred times of the year and acknowledge the natural rhythm of nature. Modern life isn't dependent on the rising and setting of the sun, but these natural rhythms of life affect us nonetheless.

Even as cultures change over time, nature's rhythms do not change. Rituals allow you to create a rhythm in your own life that reflects, is in harmony with, and benefits from the rhythms of nature.

They also allow you to create a sense of the sacred in your life. What would your life be like if you experienced yourself as sacred? Ultimately, that's the implication of your Life Design. At its transcendent core, the hidden pattern of life goes beyond the material world. Ceremonial rituals, when truly powerful, open all four gates of the Life Design. So be open-minded and expansive in your thinking, even at this early stage when ceremony may play almost no part in your life yet. What kind of experiences would you want to have from a ceremonial ritual? Here's a simple inventory that measures the growth that awaits you.

The Fruits of Ceremonial Rituals

Take a moment to check yes or no beside each item as it applies to you. We'll tell you what to do next after you finish.

☐ YES   ☐ NO   I feel loved for myself.

☐ YES   ☐ NO   I've sensed a spiritual presence I can't really explain, except that it was there.

☐ YES   ☐ NO   I've experienced amazing coincidences, or synchronicity.

☐ YES   ☐ NO   I feel that someone is watching over me and taking care of me.

☐ YES   ☐ NO   I have felt higher guidance in my life.

☐ YES   ☐ NO   I've had bad things happen that in the end turned out to be a blessing.

☐ YES   ☐ NO   I have a mystical streak.

☐ YES   ☐ NO   I believe that miracles are real.

☐ YES   ☐ NO   I believe in angels.

☐ YES   ☐ NO   I think that so-called paranormal abilities may be a lot more common than we think.

☐ YES   ☐ NO   I believe in God or a higher power.

☐ YES   ☐ NO   I believe that there are saints among us, even though they may go unnoticed and uncelebrated.

Each item is a result that ceremonial rituals are meant to create, as they have for centuries. We invite you to use your answers as a guide to the sort of ritual you want to participate in. The answers you've given are also useful in keeping things honest and realistic. If you perform a ceremonial ritual and there are no results—or not the results you wanted—move on until you find the right outcome. A bride won't automatically feel loved just because she had an elaborate, expensive wedding ceremony. No one will be certain that God is present in every church service. Seeking goes deeper than that. Feeling loved and sensing God's presence are real experiences; you can have such experiences if your intent is consistent and you trust in the process of uncovering your Life Design.

LEYMAH'S STORY

No place on earth has been more chaotic than Liberia, a West African nation that was originally founded by former American slaves seeking freedom by founding a new homeland. Beginning in 1989, clashes between repressive regimes and enraged rebels led to extremes of violence and brutality. Civil war wreaked havoc, killing a quarter of a million people and rendering a third of the population homeless. Meanwhile, 75 percent of the country's infrastructure, including roads and hospitals, was destroyed. It would be fair to say that there was blame and guilt on both sides in the endless bloodletting. The world largely turned away as the fighting was grinding down the Liberian people.

Sometimes a crisis that brings out the worst in human nature can spark the best, which is what happened with one seventeen-year-old girl, Leymah Gbowee. She was surrounded by a catastrophe of heartbreaking proportions, and yet, taking one step at a time, she galvanized a nation toward peace. The beginning was her abuse at the hands of the men who were the fathers of her two children. Leymah might have borne the brunt of this abuse silently, but instead, she was attracted by a UNICEF program on the effects of trauma, which led her to confront her own traumatic wounds. From that point on, Leymah dedicated herself to trauma care of other women victims.

She was led to the capital of Monrovia, where church programs were the most important force for peace in the country. A women's peace movement had sprung up, and Leymah became recognized as a leading activist.

As the movement grew, women came together to pray, and at one point they sang for peace in a local fish market. To an outsider, this might seem like a futile gesture, but it provided these women a direct connection with the people at the market.

Leymah knew more public attention was needed. She led a sit-in protest in a soccer field where hundreds of women wore white T-shirts to signify their desire for peace. A "sex strike" was announced, lasting several months and garnering widespread media attention. The women passed out leaflets reading, "We are tired! We are tired of our children being killed! We are tired of being raped! Women, wake up—you have a voice in the peace process!" The message was delivered at both Christian churches and Muslim mosques. Charles Taylor, the president of Liberia, drove past the soccer field every day, and soon he was forced to take notice.

Responding to pressure from the women, a peace conference between the government and the rebels was organized in Ghana in the summer of 2003, after fourteen years of war. Leymah and dozens of followers went there, too. When the talks stalled, they marched into the hotel where negotiations were being held, sitting themselves down in front of the glass door that led to the meeting room occupied by the feuding factions. They interlocked their arms to block the men in the room from leaving until a peace accord was reached and held up signs that said, BUTCHERS AND MURDERERS OF THE LIBERIAN PEOPLE—STOP!

When a peace accord was actually reached, Leymah Gbowee was greeted at home as a national heroine, and in 2005, the women's movement helped guide Liberia to a democratic election, which was won by another leader of the women's peace movement, Ellen Johnson Sirleaf. In 2011, Leymah, Sirleaf, and a third woman, Tawakkol Karman, received the Nobel Peace Prize for their incredible achievements. As you can see, rituals played a major role in bringing an end to war in Liberia, with praying, group singing, sit-ins, and other actions being united by the very essence of ritual—conscious intention. The intention to end the killing led to a whole host of possible activities. But one ritual in particular is especially moving. Gbowee gazed across the devastated landscape of her country and realized the enormous cost of protracted violence. She writes,

> A whole generation of young men had no idea who they were without a gun in their hands. Several generations of women were widowed, had been raped, seen their daughters and mothers raped, and their children kill and be killed. Neighbors had turned against neighbors; young people had lost hope, and old people, everything they had painstakingly earned. To a person, we were traumatized.

Leymah knew that peace could never be lasting until victims and perpetrators were able to reconcile with one another. She turned to the power of ritual. After the peace accords, groups of women went to towns and villages throughout the country. They explained the disarmament program that was in effect, gathering the armed men and boys with their guns and walking them to the stations where weapons were to be turned in. They waited for hours in line with the ex-combatants, and when the guns were turned over, the women initiated a ritual that was done for former soldiers, their commanders, and the warlords who had led the fighting. They bathed these murderers, rapists, and looters, symbolically cleansing them of their past deeds.

More important, they forgave them. These women, who had endured atrocity after atrocity, opened their hearts and welcomed the men and boys back into Liberian society. The ritual was inspired by the notion of "restorative justice," which builds order out of chaos by acts of mutual reconciliation. Leymah and the other women activists recognized that their country could never be whole again until its sons were once again made whole.

Although she doesn't use the vocabulary of the Life Design, Leymah was guided from a deep level of her awareness to find her life's mission. Her own vocabulary was religious. In 1997 she had a dream in which God told her to gather the women of Liberia and begin to pray. This proved to be a turning point, and throughout the coming years, her vision was always focused on God as a transcendent source and guide.

It could be Jesus, it could be Allah, it could be Buddha, but there is no way that you can effect change in people's lives if there is not someone you can rely on as the "divine intervener" or the "divine one" that you can call on every day.

It is easy to seek retribution. It is easy to pursue revenge. What is hard is to set aside the wrong that has been done to you and choose instead to forgive. The women of Liberia provided a model for every one of us. What can we create when we step onto a higher level of life, as they did, demonstrating the power of love, forgiveness, and compassion?

HOW CEREMONIAL RITUALS WORK

Rituals, when they bring healing, accomplish the same thing as therapy, but there are major differences. The first is that ceremonial rituals are performed with the intention of connecting with forces that cannot be seen. They connect everyday men and women with archetypal figures, whether they are shamanic animal guides or the moon goddess. In every guise, ceremonial rituals are actions that allow a person to go beyond everyday individuality. A woman can see herself as a goddess without being a movie star. Instead, she's going to the deeper levels of her Life Design where the vital energy that sustains everyone's existence has a universal source. A man can be a hero on a quest, even though he looked like just another commuter reading the sports page on the subway. To align with one's Life Design is the basis of all quests throughout history. Mythical heroes, male or female, are symbols for the adventure of finding out who you really are.

There are seven elements common to all ceremonial rituals that create this effect. We'll mention them briefly before talking about how they can fit into the ceremonies you create for yourself.

1. Intention. We've all gathered to participate in a special rite whose purpose joins everyone together, as High Mass creates the symbolic body of Christ or a bar mitzvah welcomes a thirteen-year-old boy into the community of Jewish adults. The intention may be held by the participants or created by the priest, elder, or pundit performing the ceremony.

This element helps provide a sense of common purpose.

2. Preparation and Purification. To have a profound experience of a sacred moment, the body must be clean and pure. Ritual bathing is often done, but there are also rites of mental purification, as when a Catholic priest formally dons his vestments and blesses the implements of Holy Communion.

This element removes the obstacles that could otherwise prevent deep experience of your transcendent center at the core of your Life Design.

3. Symbolism. Many rituals look beyond the material world to the invisible home of departed ancestors or to God. To give them visible shape, symbols are used, such as the cross or the Star of David. But many kinds of remembrances, from a bride's white gown to relics of saints, serve the same purpose, to remind the performers of the deeper meaning behind the gestures of the ceremony.

This element opens a gate to the subtle dimension of the ceremony, the part that refers to unseen things.

4. Activating the Senses. Ceremonies create their own sights, sounds, and smells, as anyone discovers who has observed religious processions that are replete with incense, music, and brilliant costumes. The five senses are totally immersed, and the atmosphere is far removed from daily life. (In India and Mexico, for example, there are villages that look stark and drab, but on feast days the inhabitants unwrap precious silks, feathers, spangles, and a host of dazzling accompaniments.)

This element engages the senses so that they can aid in the experience of complete immersion.

5. Prescriptions. Every ritual is surrounded with formal rules about when an action should be performed, in what direction to face, and often during which season. The precise order of each step is crucial if the ritual is to produce the desired effect. Nothing is haphazard, and usually the underlying reason for each step goes back to a deep connection with nature, the gods, or God. The ritual is also marking out sacred boundaries that should not be crossed.

This element allows the performance of the ritual to become automatic, so that the mind is able to transcend the thinking process.

6. Repetition. Repeating the same gesture and words over and over creates a calming effect and allows the mind to go beyond the experience of the senses. Sometimes the leader or the whole group enters a trance state in which they have gone beyond normal sensory experience. But, short of that, repetition allows the mind to dive within. This is like being immersed in a refreshing pool of water. You emerge feeling lighter, happier and more at ease.

This element allows people to rise above their everyday selves.

7. Invocation of Unseen Forces. All ceremonies turn an abstract value into something physical. "Fertility" is an abstract concept until seeds, earth, water, and sometimes blood are used ceremonially. "Purity" is abstract until symbolized by the color white, as death is symbolized by the color black. Ceremonial ritual proceeds from the recognition that there are layers of reality that go beyond sensory experience. Such rituals create a bond between the known and the unknown. By calling on a higher power, one opens oneself to receiving support from the infinite creativity and intelligence that create and maintain life.

This element supports you in being open to what you don't know, and being willing to accept help from wherever it may come.

It's the seventh element that arouses the most fascination—and the greatest skepticism—among modern people. When someone is on the spiritual path and speaks of "magical thinking," for example, the term is positive. It refers to a wide range of special mental phenomena. It's magical to think that you can bend reality to produce unexpected outcomes, to communicate with someone without words, or to have a desire and have it come true.

RITUAL PRACTICE

Places of Ceremony

It isn't hard to find a place where ceremonial rituals are performed. Even though few of us have strong ties to a traditional society, every area of the country has access to ceremonial rituals.

Clearly, churches are places of ritual, and you might consider participating through services or prayer groups. Here are some other suggestions that are highly valuable once you decide that ceremonial ritual has something to offer you:

Recovery and support groups—Beginning with Alcoholics Anonymous, support groups have sprung up that deal with substance abuse, overeating, grief, trauma, domestic abuse, and many other areas of distress. The AA model is filled with ritual, from standing up to say, "I'm Joe, and I'm an alcoholic," to the sequence of twelve steps for recovery. Consider if you would benefit from the organized support of such a group, remembering that they are open to families and other affected people besides the primary person seeking help. There is no stigma attached to attending meetings of these groups, many of which maintain anonymity for anyone coming through the door.

Men's and women's groups—Getting in touch with your gender identity wasn't an issue for past generations, but it has become one now. With high divorce rates and families in which both parents work, children are growing up with the feeling that they didn't learn how to become men from their fathers and women from their mothers. To reconnect with your masculinity or femininity, locate a local group organized around this theme. Many use rituals gleaned from myth or the shamanic traditions of Native Americans. Many people testify to how powerful the bonding can be in these groups, not just with your gender but with your family roots, ancient ancestors, and the earth itself.

Meditation groups—Almost every locale in America has a center with roots in Zen or Tibetan Buddhism, yoga, qigong, and other Eastern traditions that teach meditation and hold group sessions. For a nonsectarian group, we recommend the Transcendental Meditation technique, whose many centers open their doors for morning and evening meditation—you will be impressed by how they function as an oasis of calm and peace. Some of these, called "Peace Palaces," have even been built using the rituals and traditions of the ancient science of building in accord with natural law called Sthapatya Veda. Meditating in a group strengthens the effect over what you can achieve at home. We've already recommended that this become part of your foundation rituals every day; if you have enough time, being part of a group is even more beneficial.

Spiritual retreats—You've read about Marci, the woman who made a life-changing breakthrough when she found the courage to go to a meditation retreat that required silence for a week (see page 73). Every faith runs its own style of retreat, some focusing on prayer, others on bonding as a sacred community. You will also find that local monasteries often have outreach that allows laypeople to come in from the outside world to experience what a committed religious order feels like. Buddhist retreats are well known by now, and among any of the Eastern disciplines you can pick national centers, too, such as Naropa University in Boulder, Colorado, or the Kripalu Center for Yoga and Health in Stockbridge, Massachusetts. TM offers both national and local meditation courses that are open to anyone who has learned the technique; it's a lifetime invitation. Retreats, as the name suggests, take you away from the distractions of daily life for deeper immersion in the silence within, giving you clearer access to your Life Design at the same time.

HOW TO APPROACH
CEREMONIAL RITUALS

Ceremonial rituals are meant to put you in a place where the magical can become real. This is an area where personal experience is more important than anything else. It's realistic to hold on to your skepticism, because we live in a skeptical age. Both belief and non-belief must be tested. To assess the value of ceremonial rituals in your life, consider a few simple guidelines:

- Tradition matters. Those rituals that have survived for centuries are the most likely to contain truth and power.
- Terms such as "mystical" and "supernatural" are loaded, so avoid them. An airplane lifting off the ground would have been supernatural in the Middle Ages. Be open to the notion that the natural can expand beyond what we know about today.
- When you hit upon a teacher or group whose rituals attract you, don't be dazzled by what's on the surface. Look at the group and ask if these people have actually grown and learned from their activities. Do they actually exhibit the qualities promised to you, such as peace, a connection to God, a loving nature, or even signs of more developed consciousness?
- Don't accept group thinking. Ceremonial rituals are performed by people with a common purpose, and this easily slips into shared beliefs. Sometimes you aren't welcome if you don't accept these beliefs. Resist such pressure. Judge the group by how it benefits you. Let that be your ultimate guide.

We aren't encouraging you to be a doubter or, at the other extreme, to give credence to everything you hear. Realistically, everyone has a mixture of faith and doubt, hope and disappointment, trust and distrust inside. As you uncover your Life Design, the mixture will tend much more toward faith and trust. When you discover that your Life Design can empower and inspire you, there's less need for doubt and eventually none. This shift happens naturally through your own personal experience.

Janet's first experience when she learned to meditate brings many of these themes together. At the age of eighteen, in 1969, she decided to learn TM, or Transcendental Meditation, the technique that brought the word "mantra" into the English language. Each person was given a personal mantra by a qualified teacher, and she assumed, as most Westerners do, that receiving a mantra is a simple transaction that could be handled as quickly as getting a new PIN number for use at the ATM machine. But it turned out that a ceremonial ritual was involved. In preparation for it, her teacher instructed her to bring a few flowers, some fruit, and a white handkerchief.

"I had no problem with what Bob told me to bring," Janet recalls. "My brother had learned TM, and so I knew a bit about what was going to happen. It was called an initiation ceremony." When the day came, Janet handed Bob, her initiator, the things he had asked for.

"'Initiation' was such an exotic word. I was both scared and excited. Scared that it wouldn't work, and excited that it just might!"

She noticed that Bob, whom she knew as a friendly young man who had delivered the introductory talk about TM, was quiet and deliberate as he started the initiation ceremony, first asking her simply to sit by quietly and observe.

"I watched as Bob trimmed the stems of the flowers and carefully arranged them, along with my apples and oranges and a brand-new white handkerchief, on a gold tray. He handed the tray to me, and together we went into the instruction room.

"There Bob organized some tiny golden cups very carefully on a table covered with a white cloth. Next he filled the little cups with water, rice, and camphor. Then he put incense and a candle on the table, along with a photo of Guru Dev, whom Bob explained was the Indian teacher from whom the Transcendental Meditation technique came."

The ceremonial ritual that followed paid tribute to the teacher; made offerings of the rice, water, and camphor; and presented Janet's things—fruit, flowers, and handkerchief—as her offering of gratitude and respect. Janet watched with fascination.

"It was very simple and sweet. Years later, when I became a TM teacher myself and went to India, I realized that such ceremonies were a staple of everyday life known as a *puja*. The way I was brought up, religion was for Sundays, and the only place of worship was our church. But India has been spiritual for thousands of years, and the whole landscape is considered sacred. There are rituals for the seasons, the transitions in a person's life, and every significant event. Pujas are done at home, in temples, at workplaces and businesses— they bring ritual into every event you want to honor and dedicate to the divine."

Little of this was known to her when she learned TM that first day. She received her mantra after Bob had finished the puja. "I sat with my eyes closed, following the instructions I'd been given for how to meditate. I did this for a minute or two, so it came as quite a surprise when Bob told me I had actually been meditating for over twenty minutes.

"You're kidding me," I stammered. "I haven't been able to close my eyes for this long, ever, much less enjoy it."

We don't need to add that she became a lifelong meditator. One person's life was changed in a deep, permanent way. But what part did ceremony play? Why not hand out a mantra like a PIN number? The answer lies on several levels. On the mental level, being part of a ritual marks the seriousness of your intent. You sense that you are doing something significant. Emotionally, as Janet experienced, the space set aside for the ceremony feels special—it is an oasis of peace and calm set apart from everyday rushing around. At the spiritual level, a ceremonial ritual connects the participant to the transcendent core that lies at the heart of their Life Design. We prefer this terminology over such religious phrases as "connecting to God" or "touching the soul," but for anyone who yearns for those experiences, they occur at the transcendent core.

Janet found herself following the principles we outlined for judging the value of a ceremony. She was open-minded and extended enough trust to let herself experience whatever was about to happen. In Bob she saw someone who exhibited the qualities she wanted from meditation, such as a sense of calmness and settled composure. Her own experience was immediate and profound. She was allowed to assess everything for herself, with no group pressure. After such a great start, she was well on her way.

Certainly Janet's life isn't your own, so let's expand beyond her experience. The common thread running through every ceremonial ritual is reconnection. Parts of you that feel disconnected find a center. Personal isolation is healed through joining a communal action that is deeply meaningful to you. The following ritual practice goes into detail about how to achieve reconnection. It encourages you to begin in a comfortable, secure setting among friends and family.

RITUAL PRACTICE

Reconnection

Before they arrived at a ceremonial ritual, people in traditional societies were already closely bonded. Family and tribe gave them the core of their identity. The role of an elder was clearly defined. In modern life, such close connections can't be taken for granted. (For many, large family gatherings at Thanksgiving and Christmas are sources of tension and barely concealed resentments.) The work of reconnecting has to be done as a conscious intent; it can't be taken for granted.

You can set up a special event entirely devoted to reconnecting or use an occasion that already exists. Below is one example of each.

Birthday party: Everyone has a birthday every year; you can do something to make your next one a time for reconnecting. Before the event, sit down with some blank greeting cards and write out what you love and respect about each guest. Be brief and sincere. This is an opportunity to speak from your heart, but you don't have to gush. Suit your expression to the person you are addressing. A few words of respect would be appropriate for a boss or co-worker you don't know very well, while a sibling can be addressed with more emotion. Seal these "reverse birthday cards" and place them on a table by the door. Ask each guest to take the envelope with their name on it as they leave—in this way no one needs to feel self-conscious.

If you want to go a step further in formality, you could present each guest with a flower in a bud vase or even a small wrapped gift. (And don't feel limited to birthdays. Other special occasions, such as wedding anniversaries and retirement parties, where you are the focus of attention, would work just as well.) This is your day, and you can choose how much or little you want to reconnect. Most birthday parties are totally informal, but by adding this small but telling gesture, you are expressing your intent to bond with another person. You never know what response you'll get, but we imagine it will be surprisingly positive. You are giving your guests an opening to reconnect in a respectful and unobtrusive way.

Fireside retreat: A camping trip can be more than a camping trip when you use it to reconnect. In corporate culture, annual conventions serve the purpose of gathering everyone for inspiration and motivation. Some companies have found value in doing something more intimate. A sales team might take a weekend river rafting to cement their team identity. You can take a cue from such activities by going out into nature as an occasion for bonding.

The event can be as casual as you like, but it should be more than a tailgate party or barbecue. Set aside at least two days with an overnight. Tell the whole group in advance that there will be an evening ceremony in which they will participate, according to their own level of comfort. You are re-creating the kind of fireside gathering that exists in every traditional society, and even now you'll find that the power of sitting around a fire in the dark is considerable. If this is entirely new to you, make the group small, no more than the people you trust the most and feel closest to.

Here are some suggestions for what to do around the fire once the time has arrived:

- Assign in advance one big question that everyone is to think about before they arrive. It could be "What is your vision of life?" or "Why were we put here on this earth?"

Avoid sensitive topics, in case there are religious differences in the group, but design the questions to draw out everyone's deepest thoughts. Go around the group and have each person give a brief answer, then open the topic up for discussion. To keep the proceedings more orderly, have someone serve as moderator to call upon each speaker and keep the pace moving along, with no single person dominating the conversation.

• Find a large polished rock that will serve as the group's truth stone. As you sit around the fire, pass the stone to each person in turn, with the understanding that when they are holding the stone, they should speak their truth. This is a free-form event. Nothing is expected or prescribed. Each person simply has a chance to express something that would otherwise be hard to say; the truth stone is a ritual object for revealing what's really on your mind. (Make it clear, however, that this isn't an opportunity for venting or criticizing someone else.)

• Invite someone to serve as the group's wise man or woman. In turn, each participant asks the wise one a question that feels especially baffling or important—something that requires wisdom. You can ask a special guest to join you who has been picked for being wise—a mentor or senior executive or professor, perhaps. Or your group members can take turns performing the role of the wise one. If done in the right spirit of truly wanting to tap into your inner wisdom, this ritual can lead to surprising answers that come from an inspired source you never expected, either in yourself or someone else.

THE BEAUTY OF THE MANDALA

What would it be like to be fully reconnected? Inner and outer life would merge. In ancient cultures all over the world, there are symbols that have been said to describe the holistic pattern of life. Traditionally, they have been called *mandalas*, first in India and then throughout much of Asia. Tibetan Buddhists perform an elaborate ceremonial ritual, creating gorgeous mandalas made of colored sand, then destroying them. This symbolizes life's transient nature set against the eternal reality, represented by the mandala. You can watch beautiful time-lapse video of this ritual here: www.thehiddenriches.com/sandmandala.

Mandalas have their Christian counterpart in the form of the intricately patterned Celtic cross, in the famous labyrinth in the Chartres Cathedral in France, and in innumerable stained-glass windows that adorn every medieval cathedral. Hildegard von Bingen was a famous Benedictine abbess in the twelfth century who was prolific in music and art. She created beautiful mandala designs to describe her spiritual visions of divine energy coursing through Creation. It's for this purpose that "spiritual geometry" and other mandala-like patterns are found in every culture. Whether we're speaking of Australian Aborigines mapping out "dream time" or the intricate abstract patterns woven through Persian carpets, the hand of man was attempting to draw the design of a divine presence infusing everyday life.

Just as Tibetan monks painstakingly create an exquisite sand mandala over several days, you have the opportunity to create an even more sacred work of art over the course of your lifetime, because your Life Design is a living thing. It begins with a simple structure at birth before being filled in with all the experiences yet to come, as represented in the diagram on the following page.

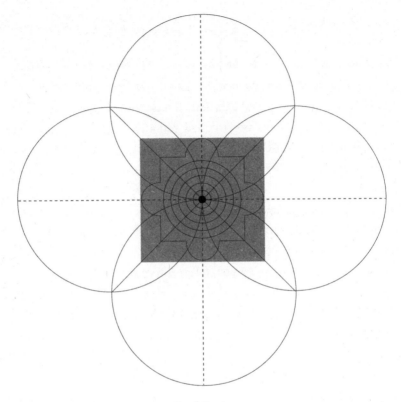

Seed Design

As you can see, this is a structure with a center and four inter-locking parts. The center is your connection to the universal, absolute part of yourself, which is everyone's birthright. It is your spiritual core (and, yes, we all have one). From here all the various aspects of what you call "me" radiate outward, like beams of light from a star. In personal terms, your light is the essence of life emerging from your core.

The four circles are the physical, mental, emotional, and spiritual—the same "four gates" incorporated into the Life Design. Notice how they are interwoven like a spiderweb, with intricacy and order. The web becomes more and more complex as it grows over the years, to the point where you might look at yourself and see your life as a tangle of disconnected threads. The beauty of the mandala— and its wisdom—is that there is no randomness once you grasp the underlying pattern. Participating in the making of mandalas has always been a way to reconnect with this hidden pattern. As they returned to their source, participants found the exact point where God, soul, and self merged into a single point. This point lies deeper than someone's everyday personality. It's the self you experience, usually in brief glimpses, when you feel inspired and uplifted.

We have incorporated the levels emerging from your transcendent core as described in ancient texts to create the Life Design diagram. Many kinds of natural connections have been lost as communal ceremonies waned. In the past, for example, when farming and herding occupied almost everyone in society, the seasons of the year were critical. Equinoxes and solstices, marking new seasons, were times of celebration and community. Each celebration connected the season with the work everyone did: tilling and planting in the spring, weeding and fending off pests in the summer, harvesting and clearing the fields in the fall, and resting and repairing tools in the winter. Traditional cultures celebrate not only the seasons of the year but the seasons of life, from cradle to grave. Here is a list of traditional times for performing rituals. Which of them do you still observe in your life?

Birth
Birthdays
Rites of Passage—transitions from childhood to youth,
    from youth to young adulthood, from young adulthood
    to full adulthood, from adulthood to old age
Weddings

Anniversaries
Building a home—laying the cornerstone, putting on the
    roof, completion of the home
Moving into a new home
Retirement
Installation as a member of a council of elders
Death

No doubt a handful of these transitions are still being marked in
your life, but if you're like most people, the ceremonies are sketchy
and rushed.

Paulo Coelho, the renowned author of *The Alchemist,* put it all
in context:

> Our time on this earth is sacred, and we should celebrate
> every moment. The importance of this has been completely
> forgotten: even religious holidays have been transformed
> into opportunities to go to the beach or the park or skiing.
> There are no more rituals.

Coelho sees deeply into what rituals once did for humanity by
lamenting their absence.

Ordinary actions can no longer be transformed into manifesta-
tions of the sacred. We cook and complain that it's a waste of time,
when we should be pouring our love into making that food. We
work and believe it's a divine curse, when we should be using our
skills to bring pleasure and to spread the energy of the Mother.

We join in this call for celebration and renewal. Modern life isn't
meant to return to its tribal origins. What we need aren't old traditions but their essence, which is what rituals bring out. Some needs
never change over time.

Everyone needs to belong.

Everyone needs to be valued.

Everyone needs dignity and respect.

Everyone needs to be part of a larger purpose.

Insofar as you can provide these things by your participation in ceremonial rituals, you are enacting a universal vision of what it means to be human. Insofar as you detract from anyone's fulfillment in these areas, you are stripping them—and yourself—of the richest gifts of being human. We're sure which way your intent lies. Now you only need to carry your intention into action.

RITUALS FOR A CLOSE FAMILY CIRCLE

The American family is rapidly changing, and you've probably found yourself in the middle of it. The traditional image of stability and love, with two happily married parents presiding over 2.3 children, needs to be updated, but in ways in which love and stability are still present. It's a challenge. Kids are growing up faster than ever, thanks to the Internet. More and more, families are becoming disorganized, with each member pursuing different interests. Many adults, having grown up with divorce, are unsure about what a secure family life should look like. We are realists and understand that families, even the most loving, are the source of stress and conflict as well as joy and satisfaction. (Now that we're older, we appreciate the joke that gray hair is hereditary—you get it from your kids.) It's time to return to the basics. What do you want your family to look like, starting today?

Family life expresses a hidden pattern. When everyone in your family is aligned with each member's Life Design, you have an ideal family. When it is out of alignment, there are blockages of energy that eventually lead to distorted behavior. Let's put this in practical terms.

ALIGNED BEHAVIOR

Every family member feels valued.

Love is freely expressed.

Children and adults respect each other's boundaries.

Daily life proceeds smoothly.

Negative feelings aren't harbored and suppressed.

Each person is free to express their feelings.

Speaking your own truth is encouraged.

Everyone is treated with dignity.

Parents and kids still get tired and cranky sometimes. There are still the normal parenting issues: kids want their own way; sibling rivalries flare up; children need to be guided to avoid potentially dangerous situations; and so on. But there is a flow to family life that makes these challenges interesting when love dominates. Then the challenges are opportunities for the love to be expressed in a variety of ways.

The situation is very different—and it is also considerably less harmonious—when family life is unaligned with its members' Life Design.

UNALIGNED BEHAVIOR

Some family members are given more love and attention than the others. Some are scapegoated as "bad" or inferior.

Love is rarely expressed. "You know that I love you" is a way of pushing someone away while giving minimal expression to loving emotions.

Children and adults don't respect each other's boundaries. The children are dragged into parental arguments and tension. The parents also intrude excessively into their children's lives.

Daily life is rocky, filled with drama and disagreements. As children grow older, they drift away into a private space and resent being part of the family.

Negative feelings are buried and allowed to fester. The result is barely contained resentment and frustration.

Expressing yourself is frowned upon. A "good" child is polite and obedient. In big and little ways parents are controlling.

Speaking the truth gets you in trouble. The truth is imposed through discipline and parental authority, where one size fits all.

There is little regard for personal dignity. Family members backbite, gossip, tell tales, and snitch on one another. Personal space is almost impossible to win.

The contrast is sharp. We don't want to dwell on unaligned behavior. Trying to solve each distorted behavior is usually futile. There's only so much nagging, pleading, and scolding a parent can do without reaching the zero point of getting results. The good news is that once you are aligned with your Life Design—and encourage every family member to be aligned in the same way—problems begin to resolve, because underlying needs get fulfilled in a positive way. A child who feels unloved needs love to flow in, not an exhausting examination of their feelings of not being loved. In the same way, the answer to any wound is healing. When the parents are aligned with their Life Design, the family begins to be a unit of healing for everyone. Life energy flows more freely, blockages are removed, and family life becomes a source of joy rather than frustration.

As the parent, you are the model who will be reflected in your children's behavior, so aligning yourself with your Life Design comes first. When your own energy is flowing, when the four gates are not blocked, there is fulfillment in each area of life—mental, emotional, physical, and spiritual. Every day brings a balance between order and spontaneity. At the core of everything is the bliss that comes directly from your transcendent center. These effects lead to alignment for the whole family. The only difference really has to do with age.

Here's a charming ritual that our friend Beth introduced to make bedtime easier for her little boy—it wound up having a beneficial effect on her, too.

RITUAL PRACTICE

Beth's Bedtime Ritual

Getting a young child to go to bed can be either a chore or an opportunity. You can turn it into an opportunity through a simple ritual. Beth tells us in her own words how she accomplished this.

"Bedtime was a hard thing to bring to a close, so we came up with the following: Every night I would tuck my five-year-old son, Antoine, in, and we would do a completion ritual. I would ask him three questions.

What is the best thing that happened to you today?
What was the worst thing that happened to you today?
What was the silliest thing that happened to you today?

"He would go into a calmer, more reflective mood as we quietly talked. Instantly there was no feeling that he was being forced to obey the rule about bedtime. Instead, he looked forward to getting into bed so that we could share.

"I discovered so many special insights through the eyes of a five-year-old. He was usually so proud about the best thing, and I could comfort him if he cried over the worst thing—the next minute he'd be cracking up over the silliest thing. There was the chance for me to guide him as he shared what he considered best, worst, or silliest. It was a wonderful way to close the evening, and he got to be completely heard. This became one of my favorite times of the day.

"One evening, after we had been doing our ritual for about two weeks, Antoine held my cheeks and asked, 'Momma, what was your best, worst, and silliest thing today?'

"The question caught me by surprise. It took me a while even to remember. I could recall the best and worst things fairly easily, but I couldn't remotely remember anything silly. In that moment I realized that I hadn't been silly enough during my day. From then on, I paid special attention to looking for silly, fun, light moments so I could share them with my precious Antoine at night. His bedtime ritual has unexpectedly changed my life."

WHAT SHOULD YOU TEACH?

Children aren't ready to plan their own lives. Their time is taken up with play, education, and early social skills. Yet in our experience, children from about age seven can begin taking the Passion Test and start getting an idea of the things they really care about. This is the first step in the unveiling of their Life Design. We had a family come to meet us in Miami, the parents and three children about five, seven, and nine. They'd been taking the Passion Test together, and each family member brought a picture they'd drawn, illustrating their passions. The parents said it was a fabulous bonding experience for all of them. When their seven-year-old son drew pictures of scuba divers, fish, and ocean scenes, they discovered for the first time that he'd been dreaming of being an oceanographer.

In adolescence a person's Life Design starts to emerge, at first in vague outline and spurts of enthusiasm for new things that may turn into lifelong tendencies. Hidden patterns are beginning to have an influence. This is a time for exploration. When parents help their teenage kids gain clarity on what matters most to them, these young adults have a basis for making good decisions. It's amazing how responsible they will be when they're clear on what they care most about.

Adults—in this case, the parents—have the chance to be role models for what it means to be aligned with one's Life Design. They are secure in themselves, and they know enough about the path to maturity that they can guide their children along it, while being sensitive to the age of each child and the path that is best suited to their fits and temperament.

Nothing about a person's Life Design is schematic; there is plenty of room for each family member to be unique in their own way. You are doing the most important thing for your family that you can ever do by aligning yourself with the hidden riches embedded in your Life Design. That step brings integrity, love, and support to your daily life—what parent could ask for more? But we also realize that behavior takes many twists and turns. Sociological studies have shown that the best-behaved children at home can be distressingly misbehaved when their parents aren't around. In one study, a hidden camera watched how toddlers behaved when they were dropped off at preschool. A little boy who looked angelic and shy, who did everything his mother said, turned into a bully the moment she left the room, snatching toys from other children and showing no reaction when they cried.

What does this tell us about children? For some, it lets parents off the hook when their children grow up to become criminals or misfits. The parents can say that they never observed signs of such behavior in the home. For others, it helps explain why two children treated with the same love and attention became entirely different people, as when one sibling became chronically depressed while the other had normal moods. At the very least, what these studies show is that home life exerts a powerful influence, but there are limits. Once a child develops a social personality, many changes take place. Which is good, too, because when we escape the nest, each person balances individual and group identity. "I wasn't brought up to lie" is a good trait to carry around from childhood, but it's just as good that children grow up not imitating the bad side of their upbringing, from alcoholism to emotional abuse.

So, where do rituals fit in? They are an important influence that you as a parent have control over. Children have unformed brains waiting to be shaped. If you can shape them in the right direction, much less will be left to chance. Consider a small thing like falling down on the playground and scraping your knee. To a child who has been taught that he is weak and fragile, the incident can turn into more proof that he can't cope with ordinary accidents—the viewpoint of a victim will probably get reinforced. But to a child who has been taught that he is strong and resilient, the incident amounts to very little.

You can use family rituals to reinforce beliefs in your children that will serve them throughout their lives (and in yourself), such as:

"I belong."
"I am loved and cared for."
"It's good to share and to give."
"I can stand up for myself and be strong."

"Living by the truth is best."

"I matter."

These beliefs are so basic that they deserve to be called essential beliefs—they tell a child how she fits into the world. We realize that parents today are uncomfortable about how much discipline to impose, about how to enforce rules, and whether there should be any punishment at all. The debate over these issues will probably never end. So back away for a moment and consider the larger picture. What is the single most important thing that your child could learn from you? For centuries the answer was simple: Obey God. Be righteous. Earn your way into heaven. Now that we live in a secular age, fewer people believe in the religious model, yet even if they don't attend church regularly, they feel guilty if their children don't learn the same Sunday-school lessons they were taught.

We would offer a somewhat different answer: The single most important thing a child can learn is how to find inner fulfillment. This, we feel, is the updated equivalent to obeying God and leading a righteous life. Here we'll offer Chris's experience to illustrate what a parent might do for a child's spiritual future.

"I have two little girls, Sophie and Tianna, and as I write, they are five and two, respectively. My daughters' mornings feature several conscious daily rituals. Sophie is very proud that she gets to pick out her own clothes before going to kindergarten. She gets a hug from her mom and me, and then her baby sister comes running straight for Sophie with her arms out wide. 'Hug!!' they exclaim together.

"This is a ritual they repeat every weekday morning. Sure, sometimes one or another of the girls is sick or cranky or didn't sleep well. Those are the times when their morning ritual is most valuable, because everyone knows what's expected. Sophie knows that Daddy will help her get dressed while Mommy cooks breakfast. She knows that I will put some fizzy vitamin C into a glass of water for her, and that when it's time to leave the house, I will carry her out the door on my shoulders.

"At the front gate we stop. I pull out my cell phone with the stopwatch function and wait expectantly. 'Whenever you're ready,' I say.

"'Start!' Sophie cries. I press the timer, and we begin the ten-minute walk to her kindergarten. During the first five minutes Sophie will repeat her 'word of wisdom' silently to herself. This is a child's introductory version of meditation. The word of wisdom is a kind of pre-mantra, and it gets a child used to silently repeating a word in the mind.

"Sophie was taught her word of wisdom on her fourth birthday. She was dressed in her best clothes and was in an excited mood. I performed a puja, or ritual offering, to the lineage of teachers, in the same fashion that accompanies adult instruction. But the explanation of what was happening was made suitable for a young child. This would be a secret word just for Sophie that would help her become wise and happy and healthy. Could she keep her special word to herself and not tell anyone, not even Mommy or her best friends? She said she could.

"By this year Sophie is quite settled and happy in the practice, which she does every morning and afternoon. After five minutes the stopwatch goes off. She cries, 'Done!' and gets down off my shoulders to walk the rest of the way. There is a ritual for this part of the trip to school, too. 'Daddy, what are you grateful for?' she asks.

"I might say, 'I'm grateful to have such a beautiful, loving family, because it makes life so much fun.' In a simple way that a five-year-old can understand, I am imparting a lesson about how much family life means, how irreplaceable it is.

"Then it's her turn. I ask what she's grateful for, and Sophie might say, 'I'm grateful that we have a house to live in, because then we don't get wet when it rains or freeze when it snows.' And so we continue, taking turns saying what we're grateful for and why, all the way to kindergarten.

"As our girls grow, our rituals change somewhat, keeping them interesting and fun. For example, when Sophie's not going to school, we still take a morning walk as she repeats her 'word of wisdom.' Then we have a little race at the end to the neighbor's wall, where she prides herself on balancing as she walks along the top of the stone wall. The gratitude game has become the 'thank you, God' game which she loves winning by being the one who comes up with the most things to be grateful to God for."

While foundation rituals like these can transform an adult's life, for those with a family, they are the ground on which your children's future is built. When you provide children with stability, reliability, regularity, and togetherness, they feel safe. By structuring regular times when the whole family is doing the same thing together, you create a sense of belonging and purposefulness that will stay with them, hopefully throughout their lives. Chris's goal is to start Sophie on the path to spiritual fulfillment, with the knowledge that one day her Life Design will bring that fulfillment.

Do family rituals really have an impact on your children? According to Drs. Mary Spagnola and Barbara Fiese, "In a longitudinal study beginning when children were aged four, families who showed a stable, high level of commitment in their rituals over a five-year period had children who showed higher scores on standard tests of academic achievement than did children of families who showed a consistently low level, or a decline from a high level of routinization."

In studies of whether eating together as a family makes a difference, researchers have found that regular family meals have a positive effect on communication within the family. Other findings pointed to better eating habits as well as improved performance in school. Following simple rituals of being together at meals also serves to decrease the likeliness of teen addiction and mental health issues.

RITUAL PRACTICE

Family Meals

For families, some of the most important rituals you can structure are those around meals. Here are a few general guidelines that will help make mealtimes something both you and your kids will look forward to.

Make it fun: As you can see in the story of Chris's family, what really holds a child's attention is making a ritual into a game. We know a couple who had a three-year-old named Sara who had begun to be a picky eater. She wouldn't touch the food placed in front of her, and the more her parents tried to coax or scold her, the more fixed this behavior became. Then they found a tip from a child psychologist.

At the next meal, her father reached over with a table knife and divided Sara's food in two. Pointing to one half, he said, "That's mine, okay? You can't touch it. You promise, right?" He said all of this with exaggerated seriousness. "Okay, I'm turning away, and if you touch it, I don't know what." The instant he turned his head, Sara gleefully gobbled up half the plate—his half, of course. They turned this into a nightly game that she loved. The father made sure that Sara knew it was a game. Every time she ate half the food on her plate, he'd divide the remaining portion in half and dare her to eat it—she always did.

At every age your kids will appreciate having some fun at mealtime. It sets the right mood for the body to metabolize nutrients, and it gives the whole family something to look forward to, even if the ritual is as simple as everyone bringing a "joke of the day" to the table.

Blessing: In Chris's family, the main mealtime ritual is singing a prayer, but you can substitute any expression of gratitude before the meal begins. This shouldn't be an empty ritual, with the words rattled off mechanically. Make it personal by beginning the blessing with "Today, we are grateful for," and then mention a particular thing that happened today. Chris will tell you that sometimes a member of the family is feeling bad or upset. But as soon as everyone sits down and starts singing, the atmosphere changes, and soon everyone is laughing again. Coming to the table in his family has become a healing moment that reassures his kids and lets them know that their upset is temporary and manageable.

A prayer or expression of gratitude is a good beginning. Make a rule that during the meal, attention is placed on things that are enjoyable, fun, and interesting—this allows everyone to feel more connected.

Many ancient traditions, such as Judaism, prescribe rituals both before and after meals, turning this time into a special time set apart from the rest of daily activities. You might consider ending the meal on a formal note, such as giving thanks to the cook and saying a few words of appreciation together as you hold hands. If everyone waits for this closing ritual, you are countering the tendency of family members to rush off to do their own thing before the meal is over.

As you structure rituals for your family, how can you imbue them with meaning, the special ingredient that makes ritual effective?

"The instruction ceremony that Sophie experienced when she learned her 'word of wisdom' helped create a sense that what she was learning was very special. It helped her feel important; what she had just learned should be treated with care. One of the values of adhering to the ancient traditions for ceremonies such as this is in setting the experience apart from the day-to-day activities of life."

Unfortunately, today many traditional rituals are performed because "that's the way we've always done it," so the meaning, symbolism, and power of the ritual are lessened or lost. This is why it's critical for you and your family to consciously design the rituals you will participate in together, thinking carefully about the meaning each element has for the family, individually and as a group.

SCIENCE AND CEREMONY

Ceremonial ritual is most effective when it brings you closer to your transcendent center, the spiritual core of your life. While the inward ritual of meditation is a powerful and proven way to accomplish this, ancient traditions include many beautiful ceremonial rituals that also allow the mind to transcend conscious thinking, but come at it from a completely different direction.

One of the markers that tell us ceremonial ritual is working is the "spillover effect" described by brain researchers Eugene d'Aquili and Andrew Newberg. They discovered that various ceremonial rituals, which activate one side of the brain, have the effect of spilling over and activating the other. Thus two aspects of the autonomic nervous system, one responsible for arousal and the other for calm, are able to influence and balance each other.

As a result, someone engaged in active, rhythmic rituals like energetic dancing and singing may experience bliss, tranquillity, and a sense of oneness.

There is also spillover from meditation, working from the opposite hemisphere of the brain. Both kinds of ritual, then, have a holistic effect. The part of your brain responsible for accomplishing things by breaking them into parts becomes balanced with the part that connects, integrates, and appreciates the underlying unity. A person experiences this as a sense of transcendence and peacefulness during tribal dancing, or a rush of energy during quieting rituals.

Rituals performed as a group strengthen the affection and connection between the members. In many families too much is left unsaid. When that happens, bonds fray. Judgments arise, based solely on silent expectations and beliefs. The damaging effect of this has been clearly demonstrated with young children at school.

In a powerful 1968 study by Robert Rosenthal and Lenore Jacobson, the expectations and beliefs of the teacher were found to have a profound effect on the performance of their students. In this study, intelligence test scores were randomly assigned to children and reported to their teachers as good indicators of each child's potential. At the end of the school year, students wound up performing at the levels their teachers expected from them rather than at the level of their actual IQ, as measured by their real scores. A silent expectation was incredibly powerful. Knowing this, you have a strong incentive to keep tabs with your child by communicating what's going on. By staying in touch with who a child really is, you won't project your expectations on them.

In addition, the intentions of the whole family will have a

stronger influence. When there is a bond between people holding a common intent, the effect is much greater than the intent of a single individual.

"Every day after lunch we sit together for fifteen minutes," Chris says, "and go over the alphabet. Sophie sits on my lap and Tianna on her mother's. We begin by singing the ancient words of the Upanishads from the Vedic tradition.

"Saha nav avatu, Saha nau bhunaktu, Saha viryam karavavahai.
Tejasvi nav adhitam astu. Ma vidvishavahai.
Aum, shanti, shanti, shantihi.

"Then we say the words in English:

"Let us be together, let us eat together, let us be vital together.
Let us be radiating truth, radiating the light of life.
Never shall we denounce anyone. Never entertain negativity.
Aum, peace, peace, peace."

The value of choosing an ageless invocation is that the words will never wear out. Two little girls may understand only a bit of what they're saying, but the meaning will deepen as they grow up, becoming the source of personal wisdom.

Rituals can be used to make your family life more interesting and engaging. They draw the family circle closer together. Outside mealtime, there are other rituals that can include friends, too, expanding the family circle—you will be forming the start of a true community, connected emotionally and spiritually. In the absence of traditional social bonds, this effort is really valuable if we want to be more connected. The following ritual gives a good example of what we mean.

RITUAL PRACTICE

Group Appreciation

Family rituals are common, even in our modern culture. If you want to enrich your time together and create memories for a lifetime, try this ritual, which can also include close friends:

When your family and friends gather for a reunion, the holidays, or a special occasion, give each person a turn to be appreciated. Go around the room and have everyone in turn say what they appreciate about that person. The only thing that the recipient is allowed to say is "Thank you." Make it extra special by having someone videotape the comments and present the video to the person afterward. In our experience, the recipient will cherish it.

At first some people may feel embarrassed to be appreciated. Many of us are so busy finding fault in ourselves that it is really difficult to hear what's good about us. We'll tend to discount praise by telling ourselves, "Yes, but they don't know such and such about me." Therefore, when the ritual is new, allow anyone who's too self-conscious to speak in appreciation rather than be the recipient. Children are generally eager for the attention, which makes them a safe place to start.

Encourage everyone to be a recipient, but if there are some people who really do not want to, let them pass, as long as they are willing to share what they appreciate about others (usually this is much easier). As you continue this tradition over time, we predict that everyone will find it so enjoyable that even those who pass at first will eventually agree to be appreciated.

Once you become completely comfortable with the ritual,

you can increase its power by having all participants gather their chairs in a circle. Put the one being appreciated at the center of the circle. This recipient's role is to look in the eyes of the person who is expressing appreciation and say, "Thank you." At first being the center of attention is like having a dozen laser beams focused on you, but at a deeper level all this attention is very nourishing and strengthening. We've known someone to squirm while being appreciated, only to express deep gratitude afterward, usually with excited exclamations like, "I've never felt this way before—it was so wonderful to hear the beautiful things people felt about me. Amazing!"

There is growing evidence that the collective attention of a group creates a measurable effect on the heart-brain connection, making it more coherent. In other words, being the focus of appreciation induces intensely positive feelings. And when you repeat the process often in your life, it will improve your sense of ease, discrimination, decision-making ability, and alertness.

Society can be transformed if people feel that they are living from their hearts, bringing a positive influence to everyone they meet. We know that such a transformation is possible, because at the family level, we see it happening already. Rituals enrich a family by creating a space for the heart, where everyone is valued, appreciated, and understood. That's the most natural way for a family to be.

Explore the possibility for yourself. A family that lives behind barriers, only partially communicating at moments when someone lets down his guard, is tragic. You don't have to pass on such a legacy. Give the gift of a new legacy—all it takes is the free flow of life energy, and now you know how to make that happen.

Part Three

YOUR
GREATEST
RICHES

HOW DREAMS COME TRUE

Let yourself be silently drawn
by the stronger pull of what you really love.

—RUMI

Why do some dreams come true but not others? In a society that loves to hear about winners, millions of people find themselves spectators to victory in the Super Bowl, the Olympics, or a mega-lottery, but what about their own victory? We've laid the groundwork for making your dreams come true, using rituals as the focus for conscious intentions. The power of conscious intention isn't really available to most people. As a result, there's a disconnect between what they wish for and what they get. So let's explore the issue more deeply.

Rituals reconnect a desire with its outcome. This happens on more than one level. Rituals are repetitive, for example, with the aim of altering pathways in the brain. Thus, they make the focus of your intentions sharper. But at the very core of ritual, there must be an emotional connection to what is most meaningful to you.

Being conscious means you structure ritual into your life consciously for the purpose of creating a more meaningful life. Intention sets you off in a direction. Emotion sustains you on the path of achievement. When an intention arises from one's transcendent center, you feel a deep passion for it (in *The Passion Test* we said,

"What you love and God's will for you are one and the same."). It is this connection to your core that keeps you focused and on track. You can't help yourself. Your intention/desire is so deeply rooted in you that it keeps coming to the front of your awareness. The intention has a deep emotional connection.

There's a wide gap, then, between "This is my heart's desire" and "My heart wasn't really in it." Emotional commitment drives a person to go beyond normal limits. When you look at Olympic runners, the first thing you notice is total commitment—running is their passion, their love, their strongest desire. But the real power of the heart lies deeper. There's a voice inside that says the following:

What I want is right for me.
This is my calling.
I can feel myself being pulled toward achievement.
My desire is making me grow.
I'm fulfilling my destiny.

These feelings are subtler and more powerful than raw desire or even passion. They come from near the transcendent center of your Life Design. This level is all but silent—its voice is beyond the level of words, operating through inner certainty instead. It's the unmistakable voice of your Life Design. When you have this deep connection, you aren't guided along a fixed path like a train on the tracks. Rather, you are guided to make choices that are right for you as a person as well as right for making your intention come true. The path is open, flexible, and unpredictable while at the same time feeling completely right—because it is aligned with your Life Design.

This chapter will go behind the scenes and reveal why rituals, even though they may play a small part in your life today, can help you tap into your own deep emotional core, the secret to turning dreams into reality.

THE FINEST LEVEL OF POWER

Life is filled with choices, large and small. With every choice, you intend something. If you carpool to work instead of driving alone, you intend to save gas, reduce traffic, and help the environment. Each aspect has a positive feeling that goes with it. Carpooling isn't your passion, but you feel that it's right. If you scrimp and save to send your children to a better college, you intend to give them a head start toward success. Here your feeling runs deeper than carpooling, yet the same rightness keeps you consistently motivated. You have emotionally matched your choices with what you want to happen. This is the power of the heart working for you.

But there are other aspects of intention that aren't so clear. Consider Olympic athletes again. When a runner wins the 100-meter dash, we can't assume that the ones who crossed the finish line after him lacked intention—they all wanted to win. They may have the same discipline, strength, and passion for running. The 100-meter dash takes less than ten seconds, yet the whole person is involved, even going beyond the years spent in training to develop a highly specialized skill. So what you see in those ten seconds represents a lot more than meets the eye.

In an Olympic race, where the difference between first and second place is measured in hundredths or thousandths of a second, one would be hard-pressed to say the difference is a result of either training or intention. If you assume we live in a beneficent universe, then at this level, the outcome is a function of the runners' unique Life Design. The athletes' particular result has emerged from their

Life Design according to what will serve them most in realizing their full potential as human beings. Sometimes being second teaches life's most valuable lessons.

This is true of all the most important goals in life. They are challenges that ultimately come down to your Life Design, and your Life Design comes down to awareness. Whether you want to win a gold medal in running, earn a PhD, or become a success on Wall Street, the four gates through which your life energy runs are crucial. When the four gates are open, your inner and outer life match. A path for fulfilling your dreams has been opened.

Let's look at some of the specifics that are needed at the finest levels of awareness. There's a rule about the power of intention. That power increases as you get closer to your transcendent center. Only here can you find that subtle feeling of rightness, the sense that you are fulfilling your destiny. Three elements come together at this subtle level of heart and mind:

Knowledge about how consciousness carries out its intentions.

Passion in directing your awareness and keeping yourself motivated.

Experience in making intentions come true time after time.

It is through the application of these three, by creating alignment between intentions and outcomes, that it is possible to have what we called "enlightened wealth" at the beginning of the book. This is a life in which all parts are rich and full.

But not all intentions are created equal. Some are impaired in one of these three departments. Knowledge, passion, and experience can all be lacking. When a small child is asked what he wants to be when he grows up, we smile at the typical answers: I want to be a fireman, policeman, nurse, the first woman president of the United States. With time, the dreams of childhood change. But some children know very early on exactly what they want to be, and years later, as adults, they testify that their intention came true. The secret isn't magic, but it is a secret. Society hasn't taught us much about conscious intentions, except through sayings like "Never give up on your dream" and "Success is ten percent inspiration and ninety percent perspiration."

There's a better way. By breaking it down, the question we started with—What makes dreams come true?—can be answered realistically and convincingly. Let's summarize the main points for each area.

Knowledge: Intentions become more powerful when they arise at a deep level of the mind. The most powerful ones are born very close to the transcendent center of your Life Design. This is the area of intuition and insight that is often more powerful than reason. There are moments in life when you stop weighing pros and cons; you just "know this is right for me." Coming from such a deep level, any intention has a much better chance of succeeding than a more uncertain intention. Once you discover a clear path to the deeper parts of your mind, you are aligned with knowledge that is more powerful than logical arguments for and against the choices you make.

Passion: Once an intention has been born, it takes passion to hold it as a steady, clear desire. An intention that drifts away on the wind is just another thought. But when there's love, inspiration, and a sense of destiny—all the living ingredients of passion—your awareness is attuned to catch all the signals of potential success that arrive every day. Then your dreams will come true far more often than for someone who lacks this attunement.

Experience: Your mind works through input and output, in a feedback loop. If you feed it with small successes every day, it will have those experiences to build upon. The more positive the input, the more powerful the output. Without repeated experience, you are like the basketball fan who gets to come on court at halftime to make a basket. You may swish the ball through the net, but a professional NBA player who has had the experience thousands and thousands of times is far more likely to succeed. In the case of intentions, the main experience comes from connecting an inner event ("I want this to come true") with an outer result ("It did come true). Once you've made this connection, the experience reinforces your belief that you can create such results again in the future. With each new success, your belief becomes stronger. When belief is strong enough, then even the biggest dreams can come true.

In the spiritual tradition of India, the triad of knowledge, passion, and experience is stated a different way. It is held that a desire or intention comes true when three conditions are fulfilled: the mind goes deep enough to be near its source, the intention is stated with complete clarity and purpose, and the person's attention is steady enough to hold on to the intention. This prescription comes from the ancient masters of yoga and deep meditation. In everyday life today, it takes a special mental framework to make dreams come true in the most efficient way. You can use struggle, persistence, and discipline to get what you want. A more efficient and enjoyable way is to use the power built into intention at a deep level of the mind. How do you know that you have tapped into this power? Some or all of the following signs will appear:

You are passionate about your goal and love getting there.
You don't meet with outward resistance and obstacles. If
    some appear, either they dissolve quickly, without undue

conflict and struggle, or the inner passion is so strong that it doesn't allow you to give up until the obstacles have been overcome. Thus, when you are in the flow of life, intentions and outcomes are connected. Even though it may take time for an outcome to unfold, the result is ensured at the source.

You aren't obsessive. Once you express your intention, you do everything you can think of to bring it to fulfillment, but then you let it go, waiting for the universe's response. (We talk about three steps in *The Passion Test*: Intention, Attention, and No Tension. To achieve no tension, you have to let go and let unseen forces aid you. Without them, the greatest goals—the ones you are destined to reach—can't come true.)

You feel confident that a path will appear to guide you to your goal, even if there are unpredictable steps, or even stumbles, along the way.

You see the purpose of every action you take, even when the immediate situation might seem like a setback. You learn from everything, including mistakes and temporary failure.

You are able to be detached enough to take a long-range view of your progress, measuring it in years if need be rather than days and weeks.

This is what it means to be in the flow of life. Most of us have had an experience of "being in the zone." Books have been written about the remarkable, almost "out of body" experiences many athletes have had when they are in this place. What otherwise would seem difficult becomes a graceful and seemingly effortless dance.

Football players report being able to "sense" opponents approaching them from behind; their body moves spontaneously to avoid tacklers; they are immersed in the rhythm of the moment.

In this state, there is an inner "knowingness" that arises and guides your activity. While modern reports are mainly of brief glimpses of this state, ancient texts suggest that it is not only possible to live in this state all the time, but in fact, this is the natural state of life.

Let's follow someone whose life turned around when she began to allow herself to step into the flow of life.

MARIA'S STORY

Maria was born in New York City into a very large Italian family with all the trimmings: a grandmother who cooked up a storm, Mass every Sunday, and crowds of cousins. Her grandfather's first job in America was pushing a fruit and vegetable cart through the streets. That cart later became a market, a deli, and then real estate. But as prosperous as the family was, Maria's father drank too much. In such old-fashioned settings the women often felt helpless and turned their backs.

If ritual is meant to solve life's difficulties, the meaningless rituals that Maria was part of had a very different outcome for her. Here everyday existence ran on a timetable of routine. Wednesday was catechism class, Saturday was for confession, and Sunday was Mass at the parish church. After Mass came a crowded family dinner with her mother's parents and a dozen cousins, uncles, and aunts. Growing up, Maria didn't think much about why she was doing these things.

By the time she was seven, Puerto Rican gangs were moving into the old neighborhood. It wasn't safe anymore, her parents fretted, so her father moved them to Long Island. Suddenly everything felt strange and new. Maria would peer out her second-floor window and watch people going by on their way to work. Connections started to unravel. It was an hour's drive to visit her grandparents, and Sunday dinners were just Maria, her brother and sister, and their parents. The big family celebrations were rare now.

The next years were tough. It seemed as if her father was always drinking, always angry, and arguing with her mother. By the time she was a teen, Maria fled the house to join her girlfriends hanging out in the local park. She was attracted to Louis, a handsome boy with green eyes and raven-black hair. He had a way of looking at her that made Maria feel he saw right through to her soul. Sometimes one of the boys would bring pot. At first she resisted, but her girlfriends said, "You don't want them to think you're not cool, do you?"

It was the sixties, and before long she began experimenting with harder drugs—first LSD, then cocaine, and finally heroin. Maria and Louis became an item. At seventeen she found herself pregnant and addicted. There was a hasty wedding. Before the ceremony, she and Louis shot up so that they could maintain the appearance of normality. That was in October 1967; the baby, a girl they named Laura, was born the following January. In April Louis got busted for robbery, trying to get money to support their habit and a new family.

After he went to jail, Maria, with no other place to go, moved back in with her mother and alcoholic father. She felt lost and alone. Her mother provided some solace, but there was no way she could tell her about being an addict. At the same time, she had to get money to support her habit, so she stole. Before too long Maria was arrested, but the judge let her off with probation as a first-time offender.

The reprieve was short-lived. Unable to meet her expenses and support her habit, Maria was caught stealing again, and this time the sentence was four months in jail. Her parents abandoned her, telling her they no longer had a daughter. Her sister visited once, which was Maria's sole contact with the outside world. She had hit rock bottom. From this point onward, Maria started an upward climb, where ritual became meaningful and supported her in unexpected ways.

Once freed, she spent a year in rehab, emerging drug free and hoping for a new chance at life. For the first time since Louis's arrest she had her own place and was able to spend time with her daughter, Laura. One night there was a loud banging at her door. It sounded like someone was going to break it down. Maria opened the door to see her brother, looking ashen.

"It's Dad. He's dead."

Her father had ended his misery by committing suicide. Confronted by her mother's grief, Maria could feel herself slipping, so when a friend invited her to a talk on meditation at the rehab center, she accepted. The fact that this was a TM lecture had some significant features.

When people think of meditation, they usually have a generic thing in mind—meditation is for becoming calmer and less stressed. But not all meditations are alike. TM specifically aims at improving a person's connection to her transcendent center, where intentions turn into reality.

Connection to your transcendent center affects every area of your life. Thus, one would expect that a technique that connects you to that transcendent center will have measurable results in many different parts of your life. That's exactly what's seen in the extensive body of scientific research on the TM technique.

The knowledge here is self-knowledge, discovering that your

mind has hidden depths from which any desire gains real power. Maria learned that it was possible—and very desirable—to go beyond the level of the mind that is tossed about by worries, habits, stray thoughts, and random impulses.

The mind, as we all experience it, is active and at times turbulent. When allowed to settle down, it experiences peace and calm. At first there's a conditioned reflex. The mind pops back up to the surface, attracted by a stray thought or impulse. There's no need to fight against this reflex, however. One secret from centuries of meditation is that the mind likes the experience of peace, stillness, silence, and bliss. If you keep exposing yourself to these qualities, your mind will say, "Ah, this is where I want to be. This is where I belong."

Maria was amazed that despite years of chaos and substance abuse, her mind could deliver the experience we've been talking about. Meditation opened a whole new world for her. It helped her to relax and begin feeling better, but even more important, she developed a new circle of friends. Their values were the opposite of the victimization that had clouded her existence for years. In time she became a meditation teacher and moved to the rural community of Fairfield, Iowa, the main center for TM in America. One ritual had effectively transformed her life. Now a second was about to effect an equally profound change in her soul.

Maria hadn't felt much meaning in the church rituals she had been brought up with, but when Easter came, she and her sister, who had arrived in Fairfield for the weekend, decided to attend Mass. Childhood rituals are deeply embedded and, even absent deep meaning, can provide a sense of security and familiarity. And so Maria and her sister looked for the chance to honor this old ritual. But when Maria called around, she discovered they had missed the local Catholic service. The only church in town that had an evening service was the Assembly of God, which was much more evangelical than anything she and her sister had ever experienced.

The preacher was passionate as he delivered his sermon, leaning forward at the pulpit and putting emotion into every word. It was as if they were hearing the story of Christ's Passion for the first time, the words going deeply into both their hearts. The sermon was about personal salvation. Jesus had died for *their* sins. Through him they could have a second chance. Maria was almost trembling, and when she looked over at her sister, whose own life had been hard, she saw that she was moved, too. The preacher invited them to ask Jesus to be their Lord and Master, and they accepted. Maria and her sister felt the release of a huge burden as a powerful energy washed through them and filled them with love.

Returning to work the next week, Maria felt her new faith as a strong, peaceful, healing force inside. With new hope, she made a commitment to put Jesus first in her life. Today her faith has an even more profound meaning for her. She's remarried; her daughter, Laura, is living a happy life in Texas; and Maria is at peace.

In this story the difference between the empty rituals of one woman's childhood and rituals that made an emotional connection is all-important. The religious rituals that Maria observes today have profound meaning for her. She has moved far away from the dutiful seven-year-old and beautifully exemplifies a quote from the late physicist Edward Teller: "When you have come to the edge of all light that you know and are about to drop off into the darkness of the unknown, faith is knowing one of two things will happen: There will be something solid to stand on or you will be taught to fly."

RITUAL PRACTICE

A Heart Opening

An inspiring part of Maria's story was how she found a way to love and forgive herself. A closed heart managed to open, allowing love to flow. The following practice for opening your heart to culture, love, and forgiveness comes from Master Stephen Co from the tradition of Pranic Healing. Master Co says those who are able to perceive subtle energy report that when a person is in love or loving another, the color pink is pervasive in their energetic field. So radiating pink energy will stimulate more love and caring in the other person.

Visualize someone you love or care about standing in front of you.

Using your left hand, tap the center of your chest. Then, raising both hands and focusing on your heart, imagine beautiful, pink light from your heart radiating like pink liquid light, flowing through your hands and flooding the other person with this beautiful pink light. Focus on your heart and recall happy events you have had with that person. Continue radiating that loving energy toward the person, imagining them in front of you.

This simple technique is used to trigger the flow of loving energy from your heart. Once the heart is flowing with this loving energy, you can visualize anyone you like (say, someone at work you're having challenges with), and as you focus on your heart and saturate them with loving pink energy, over time there will be a change in the other person.

REMOVING BLOCKAGES

Not everyone who meditates is drawn back to the faith of child-hood. That happened to be the outcome for one woman because her Life Design revealed what was right for her. She had a lot of blockages that needed to be removed first before she could see—and more important, feel—what her life was really about, but the kinds of blockages she worked through exist in everyone's life:

Old habits
Conditioning from childhood
Negative beliefs about the self
Feeling powerless
Self-destructive emotions: anxiety, anger, despair,
    hopelessness
Pressure to conform

A simple, natural desire like "I want to be happy" should find a natural path to fulfillment. When your Life Design is blocked, how-ever, the path to fulfillment becomes quite twisted and frustrating. In her past, Maria did all the "right" things in terms of finding a sweetheart, getting married, having a baby, and going to church, but these steps didn't get her closer to happiness—quite the oppo-site. Without the inner coherence of life energy flowing through the four gates—physical, mental, emotional, and spiritual—her outer life became distorted, as dictated by the blockages of her inner life.

Rituals provide a safe place for bringing up difficult feelings and then showing you that there is a path to healing. We've covered this process in our discussion of ceremonial rituals. These involve groups and communities, for good reason. When you join with other people, you don't have to stand alone while dealing with your personal demons; you see that everyone has "stuff" to confront and that healing happens more easily with support. One of the main things that keep people in a state of victimization is secrecy. Feeling ashamed and guilty, we find it too difficult to reveal our innermost secrets. As a result, they become more intense. Every victim feels alone in the dark.

For healing to occur, you have to bring the light into these dark situations. Ceremonial rituals are effective, as Maria found in church one Easter. As an individual, though, you are responsible for bringing in the light. You are doing just that whenever you re-move a blockage and open the flow of life energy, for this energy, accompanied by awareness, *is* the light. Ritual isn't a magic bullet. The power to create the life you want resides in you—in your drive, passion, and commitment to creating such a life. For many, attrib-uting this power to a higher being allows them to step out of the trap of the ego.

In the ancient wisdom traditions of the East, there are separate names for what we will call "the small you" or egotistical you and what we will call "the universal You." This universal You is that aspect of you that is connected to the deepest, most profoundly moving parts of life. It is not the consciousness of the small you, the limited you, that is so powerful. It is the universal You, the un-limited, unbounded You that you have the power to connect with, participate in, and benefit from through ritual.

What blocks you today has been built up from the past. You might walk into a new situation—meeting a possible partner, get-ting a new job, confronting an unexpected crisis—and what hap-pens? You find yourself acting the way you always do, with only small modifications. The voice of the past is telling you how to be-have. So instead of dealing with today's situation in a fresh way, you are repeating old answers, old behaviors, old solutions. Learning to see how blockages stand between you and a fulfilling life is the first step in letting them go.

RITUAL PRACTICE

Clearing the Blockage

One of the most powerful rituals in our life is "The Work" of Byron Katie. Byron Kathleen Reid (aka Byron Katie), in her book *Loving What Is* and on her website www.thework.com, describes the process she calls The Work. It's an effective yet simple process for self-investigation. Her techniques allow you to bring light into the dark places and let go of limiting concepts from the past. The basic problem the questions that constitute The Work address is rigid thinking. A belief seems to be true, and carries so much emotional baggage with it, that you can't see around it. The solution in such cases is to start playing with the stuck belief, examining it closely to see if it's really true, and then turning it this way and that to gain a fresh point of view.

The process begins by writing down a stressful thought that you think is the cause of your suffering. For example, "My husband should listen to me, but he doesn't." The Work consists of four questions and a "turnaround" that are applied to this thought. The four questions chip away at your certainty as to what the thought is telling you.

Question 1: Is it true?

In this example, "Is it true that my husband should listen to me, but he doesn't?"

Question 2: Can you absolutely know that it's true?

In our example, that would be, "Can I absolutely know that my husband should listen to me?"

Question 3: How do you react, what happens, when you believe this thought?

For our example, this becomes "How do I react, what happens, when I believe that my husband should listen to me but doesn't?"

Question 4: Who would you be without that thought?

In our example, "Who would I be around my husband without the thought that he should listen to me?"

The Turnaround

Find other viewpoints besides the one you are clinging to. Take the original thought and turn it around. Experience the opposite of what you originally believed to be true. There can be several different turnarounds. Take each one and find three specific and genuine examples of how that statement could be as true or truer than your original thought. Here are some possibilities that apply to our example, "My husband should listen to me."

Turnaround to myself: I should listen to myself.

1. I should listen to the way I'm talking to my husband. Maybe I'm not very pleasant to listen to.
2. I should listen to the problem I'm telling my husband about. Maybe I'll discover the solution.
3. I should listen to the advice I'm giving my husband and practice it myself.

Turnaround to the other: I should listen to my husband.

1. I should listen to my husband telling me that he feels overwhelmed or distracted. Maybe he's not able to listen to me right then.

2. I should listen to my husband's problems if I want him to listen to mine.

3. I should listen to my husband telling me through his actions that he's not interested. I can turn to someone who is.

Turnaround to the opposite: My husband shouldn't listen to me.

1. My husband shouldn't listen to me right now, because he has an important deadline and needs to finish what he's doing.

2. My husband shouldn't listen to me because I'm focusing on negative stuff that won't help anyone.

3. My husband shouldn't listen to me because it's not his responsibility to make me happy—that's my job.

The power of The Work is in opening your mind, freeing yourself from a single stubborn point of view. When you do that, you create what we call a "bridge of compassion" between you and those who hold beliefs that are opposed to yours. By freeing yourself from the constraints of your old belief, you allow the power of love to become a healing influence in your life.

Imagine a circle. A circle is a line connected to itself; it consists of an infinite number of points joined together. Now imagine that these points are all possible thoughts you or anyone could have. For every thought you can have, there is an opposite thought. "I like

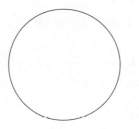

ham and eggs" versus "I don't like ham and eggs." "It's good to look out for number one" versus "It's good to help others."

If you assemble an infinite number of opposites, the circle stands for the play of opposites everywhere in life, or what we can call the "dualistic universe." For every up there is down, for every in there is out, for every top there is bottom, and so on. The Work moves you from clinging to one pole of an opposite, since the reality is always that there are two poles. That's how reality works, by the play of duality. If you can join the play, you will be taking part in the dance of life.

Each time you examine a stressful thought and turn it around, you create a bridge between your belief and its opposite, like this:

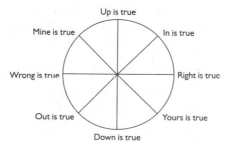

The remarkable thing about The Work is that as you ask the four questions and then turn your thought around, before long the questions come unasked. You are constantly "undoing" the thoughts that are causing you to suffer, and soon you aren't suffering from them anymore.

You can imagine what happens when *all* the thoughts you are having, not just the stressful ones, are connecting with their opposites automatically. You would experience incredibly expanded awareness. Instead of a single thought having an opposite, every thought is connected with every other, so the circle looks like this:

In this simple diagram you can envision the state of enlightenment, where the dualistic universe is replaced by unity. Opposites give way to wholeness. Wholeness carries you beyond inner conflict. To use Buddhist terminology, suffering is vanquished only when you transcend the battle between right-doing and wrongdoing. In the natural flow of life energy, right and wrong take care of themselves; any action you take is for the benefit of every living creature. This is the state of real love, where every part of life is connected with every other by a "bridge of compassion."

That's not to say that unity arrives all at once. Everyone holds on to concepts of how things should be. Fortunately, once The Work begins to build a bridge and keeps on building more bridges, the mind develops a new openness and freedom. The habit of linking opposites sets in, and once it becomes automatic, the process evolves on its own, with increasing speed and ease. The aim of love is to experience more love, until in time a state of unconditional love, directed from the core of life itself, is yours. Being whole in yourself, you will look out on a world miraculously made whole at the same time.

INTENTION CHANGES
OUTER REALITY

Let's go deeper into the simple question we started with. Why do some dreams come true and not others? For most people, the link between having an intention "in here" leading to a result "out there" is confusing. If you refer back to the Life Design diagram on page 16, the two outer rings are marked "inner life" and "outer life." They reflect each other when life energy is flowing through the four gates without blockages. Because everyone has some blockages, the flow of energy isn't completely smooth. In a word, we prevent our dreams form coming true because the mind is full of mixed messages. Think about the prospect of ordering a hot fudge sundae for dessert in a restaurant. You could easily have the following thoughts:

It sounds luscious—I'd love to order it.
But it's fattening.
I need to watch my weight.
But I do love chocolate.
How much can one little dessert hurt?

These are simple, familiar thoughts, but you can see how they contradict one another, creating a push-pull in the mind. Some of the time you'll give in and order a hot fudge sundae, and some of the time you'll resist temptation.

But what if your response to whether to order the hot fudge sundae came from a deeper level than thinking? What if you were so attuned to your body that you could feel into it, connect with your inner knowingness, and make your decision based on that rather than the rational (or irrational) arguments of your logical mind? Our educational system trains us to make decisions through logical analysis, and in some cases that's valuable, but one side effect of this training is that it causes many of us to lose the ability to connect with the subtler parts of experience beyond thinking. This is one of the values of ritual. Rituals retrain your mind to open to these subtle levels of experience.

From the viewpoint of intentions coming true, mixed messages slow down or prevent life from helping you achieve your goals. You are sending out yes/no, push/pull signals, so what you get are mixed results. Skeptics will object by saying that the outer world isn't matched to the inner world in the first place. Just because you want something doesn't mean that the physical world will respond. But a long string of experiments indicates that there is a viable link. It is validated by the wisdom traditions that have explored consciousness with as much intelligence as modern-day science's explorations of outer phenomena. Sometimes, however, the two paths overlap.

Physicist Robert Jahn is dean emeritus of engineering and applied science at Princeton University. He and his colleagues spent over twenty-five years performing rigorously controlled experiments showing that an individual's intention can affect the outcome of random events. The experimental setup was simple and elegant. A group of subjects was put into a room with a machine that generated two numbers, zero and one, at random. On a printout, the sequence being generated might read like this: 0110011011010100011. Given a very long sequence, the number of zeros would be exactly the same as the number of ones.

The subjects were asked, however, to send out a specific intention that the machine should generate more ones than zeros. By conventional thinking, such an intention should have no effect. The machine wouldn't care what was going on in people's heads; its job was simply to generate zeros and ones randomly. Yet in millions of trials the Princeton team found that human intention could create a change in the desired direction 52 percent of the time. (Other experimenters, attempting to replicate these findings, came up with a similar variance, and they even found that some people were more talented at getting the results to veer away from randomness.) While a 2 percent difference may not seem like much, it is huge for a scientist educated to believe that random means random, with mathematical certainty. Such a marked variation from chance indicates that something real is going on. But what?

To add to their mysterious findings, when the Princeton researchers had couples in a relationship hold an intention together, the results could be *six times as strong* as with a single person. Somehow a group of people with a strong emotional connection holding the same intention greatly amplifies the effect.

So now you have a strong clue about why some intentions come true. The link between the inner and outer world has to be unbroken. When there is coherence between mind, body, and the outside world, all connected by the flow of life energy, your ability to create what you want substantially increases.

Does a similar effect apply to groups having a collective intention? Here's an inspiring example.

Michael was twenty-seven. For years he'd been enjoying a remarkable and very personal experience of connection with the transcendent center of his life, which he called "God." Walking down the street, he heard an inner voice telling him, "It's time to go public." It wasn't an easy thing to hear. Although he had dreamed of birthing a new community, Michael's inner experience with the presence of

God was a personal, ecstatic, blissful thing, and part of him didn't want to give up the private, personal nature of the experience.

It took a few years before he took action. But finally he decided to form a circle, which he called a vision group, to see what it would be like to expand a personal relationship with God into a sacred space with others. He invited members of the three major parts of his life's work—his private coaching clients, students who were learning to become spiritual practitioners, and people who had attended his workshops. Those who responded met at 4345 43rd Place in Los Angeles and became a spiritual family, bound together by their love and the potential for what they might create. Together they posed the question "What is God's idea of itself, as a community, and what does that look like?"

This was an updated version of a centuries-old Christian tradition in which worshippers form the body of Christ on earth. At various periods congregations felt that their power came from praying together, but there has always been a more mystical side, where the holy presence spoke and acted through devotees. Michael's circle asked a second question as well: "What must we become, energetically and in consciousness, for this community to be birthed in the manifest realm?"

Over the following months, week after week, the circle met and envisioned what a "Beloved Community" would look like. The fruit of their work endures today, twenty-six years later, as Agape International Spiritual Center, with more than 9,000 local members and one million friends and supporters worldwide.

When he gave up his resistance at age twenty-seven, Dr. Michael Bernard Beckwith served as the catalyst to create an incredibly powerful instrument for the expression of God's will. He showed the power of creating a sacred space in which ceremony, ritual, prayer, and united intention are merged. One might also call this the power of collective consciousness when alignment with the Life Design gets amplified from the individual to the group. Agape has become renowned for its beautiful, deeply spiritual music; its close-knit, supportive community; and the powerful messages of hope and renewal it produces every week.

CREATING YOUR OWN CIRCLE

From the time humans first gathered around a fire, the ritual of the circle has been part of their social heritage. A circle can be formal or informal, or a mixture of both. Rituals cement the circle's identity. There is an expectation that one intention will be carried out, and the means to do that are agreed upon through a predictable procedure, giving all those involved a chance to add their own perspective. When we hold our regular monthly online meetings with our leadership team for the Passion Test, we begin with each person briefly stating their intention for the meeting, and we end the meeting by having each member appreciate one other member. These simple rituals don't take more than ten minutes, but they culture a closeness within the team that wouldn't be the same otherwise.

The rituals of a circle provide simple tools for giving powerful support for members to:

- Communicate honestly and openly
- Cultivate cooperation and understanding
- Encourage creative solutions
- Bridge differences
- Promote reconciliation

Just as the mandala in various forms is a spiritual symbol that appears in cultures throughout the world, the circle is a ritual that is present in every ancient culture. Obviously, we still have circles in modern life. We call them business or staff meetings. What we lack in modern circles is a structure of ritual that creates a respectful context within which meetings take place. Whether it's with your family, friends, business associates, or the teachers and administrators at your children's school, you have the opportunity to transform the nature of those meetings. We've made some suggestions in the following ritual practice. (A few practices overlap with our discussion of ceremonial rituals, but we felt that these were valuable enough to repeat.)

RITUAL PRACTICE

Circle Wisdom

In the next meeting where you feel comfortable enough with the participants to suggest it, invite the group to structure some rituals into your meeting. Here are a few that are easy to begin with:

1. Have a formal beginning and ending to the meeting. This could be the intention-setting and appreciations we mentioned above. Other possibilities: a prayer to begin and end; joining hands in a moment of silence; or reading a vision statement for your joint enterprise. Choose whatever feels like an appropriate, uplifting way to begin and end. Business meetings in particular often seem so cold and disconnected from feelings that it's a valuable practice to introduce simple things that can help the group connect.

2. Acknowledge the wisdom of the group. Every member is there for a reason. Each person contains a piece of the wisdom that the group needs to create the outcomes they're looking for.

By acknowledging this, you can create an environment in which every person is listened to with respect. For example, each person may share his or her biggest win from the past week. You could end the meeting with members sharing how they intend to put the results of the meeting into practice.

3. *Create a clear center.* Seat participants so that they face each other and mark the center with something of significance to the group. In a business meeting it could be the core values of the company, or its charter. In a family it could be a photo album or piece of family heritage. In a staff meeting it could be the team's annual goals or their personal mission statements.

4. *Create a talking piece.* This can be a stick, a stone, a gem, a piece of cloth, or anything that everyone in the group acknowledges as giving the person who holds it the right to speak without interruption. When one speaker has finished, the talking piece is passed to the next person who wants to talk. We recommend that you make the talking piece something that feels valuable. This will help remind the speaker that the right to speak is precious and that each word is valuable.

It's important to see for yourself what a circle can do when it taps into the deep reservoir of human potential. Some years ago, Janet and a few of her friends talked about how they wanted to do something through collective intention for friends and family members who were experiencing health or wealth challenges. Janet tells the story:

Our original circle consisted of myself and three others, Debra, Adrienne, and Suzanne. All of us were spiritually committed, and this kind of activity was right up our alley. We had read about the aid given to patients when they were prayed for; anyway, we loved hanging out with the unseen. Every week the four of us would meet at Suzanne's house. As soon as we walked into the room we picked a card from her angel card deck.

This is a special deck where each card depicts an angel with a little quote on the back. Over time, all of us grew very serious when choosing our angel card, because it signified what we most needed to work on in ourselves that day. Strangely, the card was always spot-on! We would then sit on the floor in a circle and put pictures and statues of our favorite religious and spiritual teachers in the middle. We'd light some incense and candles, and then hold hands as we prayed for people we felt needed our love and support that week.

When we finished praying, we'd make lunch together. More often than not, the main topic over lunch wasn't the latest movie we'd seen but how inspired our circle made us feel and how different we became, in a good way, after we met. Word spread about the experiences our prayer circle was having. Our individual lives seemed to be flourishing, and the people we prayed for were getting well and going on to lead happier and richer lives. We had tapped into something, and soon the circle expanded to eight women.

After two months of regular weekly meetings, everyone agreed that this was without a doubt the most important and significant thing they were doing. We made a group decision to meet five times a week instead of once. Debra announced that her husband had christened us "the angel group." He told Debra that when she came home from a meeting, she was filled with joy, like an angel. That whole first year we grew in our conviction that these one-hour meetings, five times a week, were somehow the most important activity in our lives.

One day after a particularly deep prayer circle, I got a call from the local high school. One of my friends had been severely burned in a fire. The school wanted to know if I would take her three young boys to the hospital where their mother lay in critical condition in the burn unit. The father couldn't be located, and the caller made it clear that the situation was grave. My friend had received severe burns over 90 percent of her body and might not make it.

I rushed the kids to the hospital and asked them to wait quietly before seeing their mother. I was anxious about what they'd see. I couldn't imagine what the sight would be, and steeled myself as I walked into the room. It was shocking: unable to lie on the bed without excruciating pain, my friend was hanging in midair, her body burned from the neck down. I was afraid that seeing her might turn my stomach, but at that moment I felt calm and accepting. The only thing that could have created such a reaction was the angel group, I thought. Over the coming weeks we prayed for her recovery, and despite the agony she went through, my friend did manage a full recovery in the end. She lives happily with her husband and three sons, who are now all grown up.

Looking back, I'm amazed at how much happened from four friends who liked to hang out with the unseen.

EXPANDING YOUR AWARENESS

Every life is multilayered. Every day you travel from waking to sleeping to dreaming. You ride the roller coaster of your emotions and play in the field of wishes, hopes, and aspirations. The ideal life is even more multilayered than the life you are leading now, because when you discover your Life Design, your life energy is free to flow. Where it will take you is unpredictable. Life is as unbounded in its possibilities as the mind itself.

In our scientific age, reality has been explored down to the finest fabric of nature and up to the galaxies. Infinity stretches in all directions. But the same is true of your inner world. Why should awareness be enclosed inside walls? Its very nature is infinite, mirroring the cosmos. When awareness suddenly opens up, the experience is like no other.

In our work, we've been fortunate to be exposed to many people who have had extended experience of the transcendent center of life. This is how one person reported the experience:

I felt very quickly access to a deeper state of happiness, which is very profound and absolute. . . . What it felt to me was like the dissolution of my idea of myself. I felt like separateness evaporated. I felt this tremendous sense of oneness. . . .

Through meditation I felt this beautiful serenity and selfless connection. I felt love. Love for myself, but also a love for everybody else. A constant state of absolute love between all of us.

Such beautiful experiences are attested to by ordinary people, and it's likely that nearly everyone has had something like them. Polls indicate that nearly half of Americans have sensed light emanating from another person, or felt what definitely seemed like a holy presence. Nearly 30 percent of responders have had a "born again" experience, and the number of people who hold what used to be fringe beliefs, such as reincarnation and communication beyond the grave, is growing steadily. Even in a society where the trend is away from organized religion, between 80 and 90 percent of people report that they believe in God, the soul, and going to heaven after they die.

EBEN'S STORY

Why was he awake? It was four-thirty in the morning, an hour before Eben needed to start getting ready for work. As he lay in bed, he noticed a pain that got steadily more intense. Swinging his feet out of bed, Eben stood up—the dull, throbbing pain shifted to the base of his spine. His wife was still asleep, so he quietly eased himself down the hall to the bathroom, thinking that a warm bath might help. It had worked before when his back ached. Gingerly he slid into the water, anticipating its soothing effect, but the pain only grew worse. It wasn't like anything he'd ever experienced before.

Eben was a doctor, and as he eased himself into a bathrobe and crept back to the bedroom, his mind rummaged through a catalog of possibilities before he collapsed on the bed. Soon he was losing consciousness, and his wife rushed him to the hospital where he worked, but within the hour a medical tragedy unfolded as he went into uncontrollable convulsions.

Dr. Eben Alexander was an accomplished neurosurgeon who had spent fifteen years working at Harvard Medical School and Brigham and Women's Hospital in Boston. Wanting to be closer to their families, in 2006 he and his wife had moved to Lynchburg, Virginia, to work at the Focused Ultrasound Foundation in Charlottesville. He was well known to practically everyone in the local medical community.

The attending, Dr. Laura Potter, tried without much success to get Eben's seizures under control with a lumbar puncture while six nurses and orderlies held him down. It took some time to arrive at the grim diagnosis: bacterial meningitis, a rare condition caused by a virulent strain of *E. coli*. The disease attacks fewer than one in ten million people. Over the course of a week, the cerebral cortex, the outer portion of Eben's brain, completely shut down. He lapsed into a coma that lasted seven days, and his chances of survival went from 10 percent to 3 percent as each day passed.

The only parts of his brain that continued to work were the primitive regions that maintain bodily functions. From the perspective of modern medicine, the part of Eben that could think, dream, imagine, calculate, or even hallucinate was dead. It would be impossible to credit that he was having a life-changing vision that would catapult him to public attention.

Eben Alexander's extraordinary journey, as related in his 2012 bestseller, *Proof of Heaven*, joins hundreds of accounts of "going into the light," in which a patient has died in the ER or on the operating table and then come back. It stands out, however, on two counts. The first is that Alexander wasn't just a doctor but a neurosurgeon, well equipped to know how the brain functions at extreme limits.

Secondly, he details a journey to heaven that is incredibly rich in detail—this from someone who didn't believe in the existence of heaven.

Since his book created such a sensation that many readers will already know it, we won't retell the whole story. But he, like many survivors of near-death experiences, returned with a deep sense of peace and a certainty that he had seen deeper into reality than ever before.

He was surrounded by darkness, but not pitch-black darkness. He was aware that he existed, but without memory of his family, his work, his life, or who or what he was. All he knew was that he was "here," wherever "here" was.

As he got his bearings, what he experienced was filled with a beauty, magnificence, and wonder he later realized he could never fully describe. There was no sense of time, but at some point he noticed that he had a companion, a lovely girl, flying beside him. Golden-brown curls framed her high cheekbones and deep blue eyes. As she looked over at him, her gaze made every moment of life worthwhile. It wasn't romantic or even the look of a dear friend. It was a deep, penetrating look filled with a love that surpassed anything Eben had ever experienced.

He then became aware that the two of them were being borne on an intricately patterned surface, bursting with dazzling colors—they were riding on a butterfly! The girl began to speak without words, the meaning passing through him with the force of immediate truth. Eben describes three messages insofar as they can be put into words:

"You are loved and cherished, dearly, forever."
"You have nothing to fear."
"There is nothing you can do wrong."

Eben felt a wave of relief, as if he'd been playing a game his whole life and someone finally explained the rules. Countless remarkable events ensued, but what penetrated deeply was this message, as it continued after he woke up, against all odds, from his coma, and he fully recovered brain function. Dr. Alexander's account was met by some—mostly professional debunkers—with skepticism and controversy. We aren't detailing the arguments from both sides, since they represent hard and fixed positions. We've accepted Alexander's account at face value because it echoes and supports so many other near-death experiences.

You may wonder why we consider this story an example of expanded awareness, since on the surface it may appear to be religious, a confirmation of heaven as a reality—Alexander felt that the existence of God was now a certainty. Our answer returns to the Life Design. What almost every near-death experience contains is a sense of freedom and expansion beyond boundaries. The doubt and confusion of everyday life are replaced by certainty and clarity. That's exactly the kind of transformation that occurs when your life energy is no longer blocked. With freedom comes a completely new reality. Without saying yes or no to Alexander's "proof" that he went to heaven and came back again, there's a striking similarity between the knowledge he gained and the level of Knowingness in the mandala of the Life Design.

On his journey, Alexander found that many questions came to him, and they were instantly answered, without his using logic, reasoning, or even words. The answers took form inside his awareness as an explosion of light, color, and love. The experience brought a profound sense of knowing. Each answer contained a totality—all at once he could see everything related to the question. As he looked back on it, Alexander realized that in a flash of insight, he gained an understanding that would have taken years to grasp on earth. But if we strip away the intensity of what happened, its spiritual overtones, and all the enticing color and beauty, something familiar occurred. The "Aha" of insight is a universal experience. Insight and imagination, the sudden inrush of love, moments of ecstasy—these are essential aspects of awareness.

If you take this angle on Alexander's story, the whole point is to tell us who we are, here and now. His journey wouldn't seem unusual to an enlightened master or Christian saint or advanced yogi. They have all experienced the intensity of awareness that comes about when the Life Design fully emerges. What is revealed can be called God, but it can also be called fully expanded awareness, or pure awareness.

It's not necessary to go to heaven to experience the love that pervades everything, including the smallest details of everyday life. A state of expanded awareness brings this love to light, as expressed beautifully by Kahu Kawai'i, a Hawaiian kahuna, or shaman: "How you might feel toward a human being that you love is how you might feel toward a dry leaf on the ground and how you might feel toward the rain in the forest and the wind. There is such intimacy that goes on that everything speaks to you and everything responds to how you are in being—almost like a mirror reflecting your feelings."

The sense that outer life reflects inner life is a major sign that you are fulfilling your Life Design. Two aspects of awareness that we generally accept as separate in fact are united when you begin to live from the transcendent center of your being.

HIGHER DIMENSIONS IN EVERY TRADITION

For centuries the journey to other dimensions has been made time and again. Through these journeys people found new ways to see where human beings belong in the vastness of creation. Rather than speaking of gods and goddesses looking down from many heavens, we equate higher dimensions with higher consciousness. Ceremonies to the gods were two-way communications. The participant asked for gifts and favors; the gods either sent them or did not. But in the world's wisdom traditions, there isn't really a two-way dialogue. We speak to other dimensions of ourselves. The gods and goddesses are convenient images for the qualities of human awareness, the very qualities brought out as you unfold your Life Design.

One assurance that we have is that the traits of higher consciousness are described in the same way in cultures East and West. Separated in time and space, the inner voyage still arrives at the same destination. Following are some of the names given to these traits across a variety of traditions. The names are different, but the essence is the same. What if all these different traditions are in fact describing the same reality, just using different words?

Wisdom—The archangel Uriel in the Judeo-Christian tradition; Thoth In Egyptian culture; Athena in the Greek tradition; Minerva in Roman culture; Saraswati in the Vedic tradition; Asi in Persia; Mimir in the Norse tradition; Emer in the Celtic tradition; Omoikane or Fukurokuju in Shinto tradition; Erlang Shen in China.

Justice—The archangel Michael in the Judeo-Christian and

Muslim traditions; Aino in Finland; Akonadi in Ghana; Ma'at in Egypt; Belet Seri in Babylonia; Justitia in Roman culture; Varuna in the Vedic tradition; Themis in Greek; Forseti in Norse; Itztla-coliuhqui in the Aztec tradition.

Healing—Ah Unicir Dz'acab in the Mayan tradition; Sekhmet in Egypt; Asclepius in Greek tradition; the Ashvins in Vedic cul-ture; !Xu for the Bushmen of Africa; Patecatl in Aztec tradition; Wong Tai Sin in China; Raphael in the Judeo-Christian traditions; Israfil in Islam.

Divine Messenger—Mercury in Roman tradition; Hermes in Greek culture; Gabriel in the Judeo-Christian and Muslim tra-ditions; Agni (also lord of fire) in the Vedic tradition; Elégbara in Yoruban culture; Hahana Ku in Maya tradition; Ismud in Mesopo-tamia; Mlentengamunye Swazi in Swaziland; Ockabewis among Chippewa Indians.

Prosperity—Anauel in the Judeo-Christian tradition; Aje in the Yoruban tradition of Africa; Daikoku in Japan; Tsai Shen in China; Lakshmi in the Vedic tradition of India, Euthenia among the Greeks.

INNER GUIDANCE

Many ancient cultures describe levels of the celestial realms, just as we see the levels of existence in our world, from primitive single-celled organisms to higher primates and humans, each with their own scope of intelligence. Science has organized intelligent life-forms in hierarchies from least intelligent to most intelligent. It's not that big a stretch to imagine that this continuum of intelligence could continue much farther, to include levels of life beyond ours, existing in dimensions not accessible to our senses. In fact, many religious and spiritual traditions describe hierarchies of angels or devas or other more intelligent beings that represent a higher level of development than humans.

For a Christian, the celestial dimension is envisaged in forms appropriate to Christian beliefs—the risen Jesus Christ, angels, the throne of God, a landscape with all the beauty of paradise. The imagery won't be the same for Hindus and Muslims, but that doesn't matter. What Eben Alexander experienced was sudden access to truths that lie deep within; there is no reason to believe that the particular imagery he experienced would be everyone's experience. It's just as likely that his experience of the nature of life was universal, expressed in images that would be meaningful to him. It fit his expectations and hopes; his personal vision of God was most likely an expression of how the deepest part of his individual nature was able to understand what is beyond human understanding.

Whatever path you follow, the purpose is to lead you to the same core of truth that Eben Alexander found, where fear is dissipated, love is revealed, and the workings of light and darkness, good and evil, God and human, are unfolded in the mind as the facts of existence, as much as gravity and the laws of nature are facts, invisible to the naked eye. Rituals serve to demarcate the path with visible symbols and organized gestures that show the mind where it must go next.

We've described many ritual practices in this book. They are intended to lead you to evolve and grow. The externals of the rituals look different, but the inner goal is always the same. So how do you know if you are actually reaching the goal? Nature will guide you, meaning that your own inner wisdom will signal you. This is the most reliable guidance anyone can follow.

When people seek guidance, they usually feel confused and conflicted. They are pulled this way and that. We all find ourselves in situations when the way forward simply isn't clear, and until there is clarity, we naturally feel anxious and doubtful. If there is any part of your life that makes you feel this way, here's a ritual to acknowledge it, learn from it, and then realign with your Life Design. We call it "Nature's Guidance System."

The foundation of this guidance comes from your own experience. We've all had the feeling of being expanded and the opposite feeling of being contracted. They happen all the time. Sometimes you feel great, on fire, passionate, energized, excited, loving, generous, and optimistic—this is the state we refer to as "expanded." Other times you feel down, lonely, anxious, worried, angry, frustrated, irritated, exhausted, depressed, and pessimistic—we collectively call this state "contracted."

Not all of these feelings need to exist, nor do they have to be intense. Most people, assuming that they don't have a history of depression or anxiety, fall into the middle range of mild to moderate negative moods. The day is going normally when suddenly there is a reason to contract, to draw into their shell. They get bad news or a big credit card bill arrives or the school calls wanting a parent-teacher conference. Whatever the trigger, they no longer feel open, relaxed, and easy about things.

When you are conscious of this uncomfortable shift, you have a choice to use it for your benefit. But most people simply react without thinking, trying to avoid the pain or discomfort by throwing themselves into work or overeating or running away, even to the point of alcohol or drug abuse. These attempts to avoid uncomfortable feelings simply bury them below the surface, only to rear their heads later. That's why a condition like mild depression can begin to spiral into a more severe form as triggers get repeated and reinforced. This spiral has been building out of sight, often without being noticed. Is it any wonder that the use of antidepressants increased 400 percent between 1988 and 2008? They don't cure the underlying condition and are increasingly needed to suppress it.

If you imagine that life exists on a continuum from joy and fulfillment to misery and suffering you can imagine Nature's Guidance System working like this:

NATURE'S GUIDANCE SYSTEM

Joy and Fulfillment

Red Light   Green Light
●   ○
Contraction   Expansion

Misery and Suffering

Life is filled with expansion and contraction. It's just like breathing. Sometimes you breathe out and sometimes you breathe in. Both are necessary for life to continue. The same is true of expansion and contraction, no matter how much you might think you want to feel expanded all the time.

Depression arises when someone experiences contraction and focuses on the story they think caused that contraction. "What you put your attention on grows stronger" means that the more you give attention to what you think makes you miserable, the more miserable you will become, as indicated by the downward spiral on the left of the diagram above.

But expansion and contraction happen to everyone—even people who are incredibly happy and successful. So what's the difference? It's all in how they interpret their experience.

When you begin to realize that contraction is just a signal to stop, take a break, and gain more clarity, then you stop suffering. It's just like a red light when you're driving. If you are wise, you don't resent the red light. You realize it's there to save you from an accident and ensure the smooth flow of traffic.

In the same way, periods of expansion aren't personal. They are like the green light that tells you it's time to go, take action, follow your passions and pursue the direction that inspires you.

RITUAL PRACTICE

Nature's Guidance System

The following practice is an easy, effective way to return to expansion as quickly as possible whenever you feel contracted:

The Expansion Process

Step 1: Notice what's going on inside. Until you become conscious that you are contracted, there's not much you can do about it. So be alert, and don't shrink from the symptoms of contraction, which include the following:

Gloomy thoughts appear.
Your mood is no longer cheerful and optimistic.
You have started to worry.
Getting anything done becomes a major chore.
You get a sinking feeling in the pit of your stomach.
You feel alone and helpless.
You have a vague, troubling sense that something bad is
    going to happen.
Sadness sweeps over you, often unexpectedly.

You feel stiffness or discomfort somewhere in your body, such as abdominal tightness or a stiff neck.

You feel sore at heart, usually with tightness or pain in that area.

Actual pain appears, such as a headache or stomachache.

Step 2: Breathe. Once you notice any sign of contraction, pause and take a few deep breaths. Close your eyes and feel your breath reaching deep inside, opening up your whole physiology. Allow a sense of relaxation to spread. Whenever we get upset, our breathing will tend to become shallow and irregular, so breathing deeply will help you to settle down. There is no more powerful mechanism for resetting the body at every level.

Step 3: Ask to be open. When you're contracted, are you more likely to say yes or no when someone asks something of you? No, of course, even when the thing you're saying no to could be help and support—just what you need to feel better. So, go inside and say, "Please allow me to be open, to expand again." Here you are setting your intention in the right direction. At the same time, you are acknowledging to yourself that expansion is your natural state.

Step 4: Go into the feeling. Once you feel a bit more settled, you need to release the discomfort and tightness that is causing you to contract. Generally this comes down to either a physical or emotional sensation or negative thoughts. Whatever the feelings associated with being upset, they are asking to be felt. If you shrink away instead and bury the discomfort, it will generally increase in order to get your attention. You aren't being punished when this happens. A part of you wants your attention.

Because they can be painful, most of us try to avoid stressful feelings. But avoidance will only make things worse later. Say to yourself, "These thoughts/feelings/sensations want to leave. I can show them the way out." Go to a private place and feel the specific stress—mental, physical, or emotional—being focused but easy.

There's a certain skill at doing this that develops with experience. Most people approach a stress with low expectations, worrying that an isolated symptom points to a huge problem that will be too fearful to confront. Certainly everyone's discomforts fall into a pattern. If you tend to get depressed while someone else gets angry, if you feel butterflies in your stomach while another person gets a headache, your uniqueness will become familiar over time. This sense of "here we go again" masks the fact that the negative feeling, thought, or sensation, no matter how often you've experienced it, still wants to leave. The body-mind system is set up to discharge pain and discomfort. So don't get discouraged—you can't discharge years of conditioning all at once. It just takes persistence and the knowledge that you can be expanded if you want to be.

Caution: We are not advising you to simply feel the pain of a medical condition to make it go away. There's a huge difference between feeling heart sore and having a heart attack. Persistent physical symptoms, especially if they grow stronger over time, absolutely require a doctor's care.

Step 5: Feel the sensation. As you are paying attention to the source of your discomfort, keep breathing. Only this time, consciously breathe the discomfort away. Let it ride out of your system on the exhale. Notice any physical sensation in your body and allow your attention to go to that sensation. Many people find that visualization helps here—they see a white-gold light filling up the body and then flowing out on the exhale, carrying any negativity or impurity with it.

Remember, your feelings belong to you, no one else. Let them go where they want to, while staying within your comfort zone. In the present moment, most people can release only a certain amount of emotion—there's little chance that your anger will boil over into rage or your sadness into despair. Here's where practice comes in handy. Release a little bit of emotion the first time, feeling your way gradually. Making noise is useful: shouting into a pillow, groaning or moaning, crying aloud. Your emotions know the sound they want to make. Allow them to. The same goes for bodily movements. There's release in swinging your arms, stamping your feet, jumping up and down, and kicking the air.

Don't force any of these release mechanisms. This isn't about drama but about sensing what your system wants to do in order to release its discomfort. Keep going until you feel that the contraction is letting go and expansion is setting in. Don't release your stress so forcefully that you are drained at the end. The secret here is that once you signal to body and mind that you want to release a stress, taking the first step is usually enough to trigger a process that your system will continue on its own.

Step 6: Use the tools. Follow up by using the tools you have to return to a more expanded state. In this context, tools are anything you know will help you feel better. It could be going for a walk, listening to music, talking with a friend, doing The Work of Byron Katie, or any other tool you're used to using. Just be alert to feel the feelings *before* using these tools; otherwise, they become yet another way to avoid feeling the source of your contraction, which will then get stored instead of released.

Step 7: Communicate clearly. If the upset has to do with some-one else who's close to you, the time to talk to them isn't while you're still feeling upset and contracted. An immediate confronta-tion will always lead to more contraction. Wait until you're feeling more expanded and at ease. Now you can approach the other person more lovingly, with a better chance of making a difference.

We use a three-part formula for clear communication. It's incredibly valuable in relationships with spouses, partners, family, and friends. It can even be adapted, using appropriate wording, to colleagues and bosses at work. In its pure form, the three-part formula is "I love you and I love me," but you can modify it to fit the situation: I value you and I value myself, I respect you and I respect myself, I hold you in great esteem and I have high self-esteem.

Here's how it works:

1. *I love you.* Begin by expressing what you appreciate and value about the other person, showing that you under-stand and respect their perspective.
2. *And.* "And" connects, "but" separates. Ever have some-one say something nice to you that continues with "but"? It wipes out everything said before, doesn't it? Use "and" to create a different expectation.
3. *I love myself.* This is a point of mutual respect. Clear communication requires sharing what your needs and expectations are. When you stand upon your own self-esteem and dignity, you create the chance to arrive at a conclusion that can work for both you and the other person.

The value of Nature's Guidance System is that you are aligning with your own nature, the tendency for the body-mind system to reach balance, comfort, and lack of stress. You can see the same in animals, as when a cat fails to catch a bird. It walks away twitching its tail and then takes a nap, two mechanisms for releasing frustration that come naturally to it. Human beings aren't so different. We shake off a bad mood and shrug at minor problems. We feel better emotionally after taking a nap. In the ritual we've just given you, such natural reflexes are taken a few steps further.

Getting out of contraction takes practice but is well worth it. Everyone needs supportive tools; there's too much stress out there to try and shrug it all off. Every day for the next week, make a mental note when you get upset, irritated, frustrated, angry, or exhausted. "Ah, this is what contraction feels like." Become acquainted with the rhythm of contraction and expansion that follows you throughout the day. It can be expressed in pairs:

CONTRACTION VERSUS EXPANSION: OPPOSITE POLES

To know where you're coming from, you have to name what's going on. Without a label, feelings simmer and get nowhere. Anytime you begin to detect that you're starting to contract, even if the feeling is vague, consult the following list and name your discomfort. Once you know the situation inside, you can change the situation outside. Self-awareness is the key to expanded awareness.

Irritable versus contented
Sad versus cheerful
Painful versus pleasurable
Stressed versus relaxed

Tight versus loose
Stiff versus flexible
Hard versus soft
Pessimistic versus optimistic
Open-minded versus closed-minded
Controlling versus allowing
Demanding versus tolerant
Frustrated versus satisfied
Rejecting (no) versus accepting (yes)

Once you've gotten used to how these polarities work to make you contract or expand, start focusing on our own particular pattern of contraction. Make a list, and then use the Nature's Guidance System ritual to get out of your contraction. With practice, this is a powerful way to become more expanded overall.

My typical states of contraction

1._____
2._____
3._____
4._____
5._____

By focusing on inner guidance, we seem to have wandered a bit far from rituals, but in reality that's not so. From India to the Americas, when you witness a ceremonial ritual from the outside, you typically see chanting, dancing, offerings, smoke, and distinctive body markings. But what is really happening on the level of consciousness goes beyond the physical—an inner connection is guiding the participants on their journey. They may go into the celestial or subtle realms that Dr. Alexander describes so vividly. There may be contact with spirits, animal guides, or departed ancestors. Or there may be nothing visual at all. Instead, they could be contacting the level of knowingness that Alexander visualized as a ball of light, the orb that taught him higher truths.

Behind the dancing, chanting, and rising curls of smoke, the participants in rituals that go back thousands of years could be experiencing profound states of consciousness. Here's one description of the experience of ceremonial ritual from Tlakaelel, or "Toltec elder," the name adopted by Francisco Jimenez as he pursued the ancient ways of pre-Columbian Mexico for fifty years:

> . . . inside there, you reach a point where you feel ecstasy. It's a very beautiful thing, and everything is light. Everything is vibrating with very small signals, like waves of music, very smooth. Everything shines with a blue light. And you feel a sweetness. Everything is covered with the sweetness, and there is peace. It's a sensation like an orgasm, but it can last a long time.

Ceremonial rituals are designed as mechanisms to connect with higher levels of guidance. When you make a connection, you touch upon the same truths that the greatest spiritual teachers convey and that Alexander discovered when he journeyed to the core. There is guidance inside all higher knowledge. Your awareness allows you to access this knowledge to solve problems, reach a cherished goal, or simply continue to evolve. When you begin to access your own deeper intelligence, you realize that fear is unnecessary, "evil" is limited, and, above all, you are loved.

These are not just platitudes. Today research published in peer-reviewed journals supports the idea that such profound inner experiences have an influence far beyond the individual.

In a series of experiments with large groups practicing TM together over a set period, usually around a week, researchers were
able to study the crime statistics, and indeed, in every case where
groups were meditating in a large city, crime rates decreased pre-
cisely during the set period in question—crime was higher both before and after the experiment. Inner peace and outer peace seem to
be matched.

In one of the most dramatic examples of this effect, published in
the *Journal of Conflict Resolution*, a group of advanced TM meditators practiced their program in Israel for several months during the
Israeli-Lebanese war in 1983. Researchers measured the relationship
between the size of the group of meditators and a number of vari-
ables, including the number of war deaths in Lebanon. They found
a direct, inverse relationship. When the size of the meditating group
increased, the number of war deaths dropped, and when the size of
the group went down, war deaths went up. Using the most sophisti-
cated statistical analysis available, they ruled out every conceivable
alternative explanation for these results. Reportedly, when one of
the reviewers returned the paper to the journal, they commented,
"There is no way I can believe the findings of this study, but the
scientific method is impeccable, so I can only recommend that it be
published."

It is hard sometimes to believe that things beyond the reach of
our senses and outside the realm of the material world are real.

Yet when we adopt a different perspective, that the transcendent
center of each person's life is connected to all life, then research results like those in the *Journal of Conflict Resolution* make sense.

Today, more than ever before, the evidence is irrefutable that
our inner world affects the outer world. This inner world leads to
new discoveries that emerge as your Life Design unfolds. They aren't
reminders to be taped to the bathroom mirror. Inner and outer life

must evolve in order for truth to take hold and become a living part of you. Can you imagine that an inner connection might be different from the kind of communication you are used to, which comes from the outside? Most of us are so used to external influences that we don't see how they close us off from our own inner knowingness. We all accept secondhand opinions and beliefs. We fall into the habit of thinking the way everyone else thinks. The pressure to conform makes it hard to go inside and find your own truth. Someone might find out and tell everyone else how different you are. But the inner journey is the most fantastic voyage you can imagine.

GLIMPSES OF EXPANDED AWARENESS

There is no reason to think that "higher" experiences are reserved for a select few—we all have a Life Design that is part of our being and is leading us inexorably on to know the deepest aspect of our own nature, from which such experiences typically emerge. Many times, often without noticing it, you have glimpsed the open, expanded, blissful state that arrives when you touch the transcendent center of yourself. At other times you touch different levels of your Life Design—for example, you access Knowingness when you have a flash of insight or intuitively know that something is true.

Take a moment to write down and validate that you have had such moments of expanded awareness. By noting them here, or in a journal, you will become more aware of these special moments and make them a conscious part of what you expect from your life.

1. Think of a time you felt bliss or a deep sense of joy or ecstatic happiness:

_____

_____

_____

2. Think of a time you had that inner "knowing," that gut feeling, when your intuition was right on:

_____

_____

_____

3. Think of a time when you were really present and in the moment; a time when you felt a deep connection to others around you:

_____

_____

_____

4. Think of a time when you felt a deep sense of peace and perhaps even others noticed how peaceful you were:

_____

_____

_____

As you connect to your own inner wisdom, the "higher" levels of intelligence are reflections of yourself. But, as with Alexander's glimpse of other dimensions that cannot be known until one enters them, the layers of wisdom at your core, which can provide all the joy, creativity, and truth that you are meant to live, can be glimpsed only when you fully enter them. To try and conceive of infinite intelligence is as impossible as conceiving of infinite universes. But the actual setup is that infinite intelligence develops a unique path for each person. This uniqueness means that you don't have to cast around looking for truth out of a vast storehouse of the world's wisdom traditions. You have to look in only one place, which is within, at the transcendent center from which all levels and layers arise. This is the reason meditation, the ritual of systematically transcending thought, is at the core of these wisdom traditions.

At the end of a week, Eben Alexander sat up in bed in the ICU, a return that was medically astonishing. He had survived a disease that has a 97 percent mortality rate. He woke up with a full memory of what had happened while he was in a vegetative coma, which rarely happens. He proceeded to defy medical expectations by regaining a state of normal health. (His sister even described a rainbow that appeared over the hospital when she came to visit the ICU that day, unaware that her brother had just woken up.)

But for him personally, the greatest surprise was his transformation from a skeptic to a proponent of near-death experiences. At first he wasn't ready to accept that his experience had happened for a reason. "There was enough of the old doctor in me," he writes, "to know how outlandish—how grandiose, in fact—that sounded." But the weight of impossibilities, one after another, became too strong.

> . . . when I added up the sheer unlikelihood of all the details— and especially when I considered how precisely perfect a disease like *E. coli* meningitis was for taking my cortex down, and my rapid and complete recovery from almost certain destruction—I simply had to take seriously the possibility that it really and truly *had* happened for a reason.

Eben's journey to heaven mirrors the journey of life that all of us are on, moving from where we are to a place where love can be experienced as a law of nature and the foundation of life itself.

As you clear the rubble and begin to have access to the infinite potential at the center, your experiences will become the beautiful, unique expressions of you. Living your Life Design will be an inspiration to others. It can be visualized like this, a radiant design that truly expresses your hidden riches:

The Expressed Life Design (Art by Joma Sipe)

In this gorgeous work by Portuguese artist Joma Sipe, the center is expressed through the four gates that are now linked by the two rings of Inner and Outer Life enclosing them. This is a life that contributes richness and encouragement to everyone you come into contact with.

Our book ends where your journey begins. Looking back, you'll see all kinds of rituals for improving your life. They can be summarized as a 3 + 1 structure:

The three fundamentals of daily life: time, energy, and mind;
Plus the spiritual dimension, where everything finds its infinite source.

The ultimate purpose of your Life Design is to welcome you into wholeness, into "enlightened wealth." You'll see for yourself that separation is just an appearance generated by your senses. When your awareness expands fully, reality shifts. There is only love and connection. The world is made whole when you are made whole. Since wholeness is the simplest state of existence, it causes the complicated problems born of the sense of separation to fade away like mist. You will see, perfectly and clearly, that your life is supported by infinite creativity, intelligence, and, above all, love. A never-ending story turns the next page, and human life really begins.

POSTSCRIPT:
THE WORLD CALLS,
CAN YOU HEAR?

It is after sunrise, and the young man is called to emerge from the cave that has been his home since infancy. He's excited, filled with anticipation. He walks slowly to the ridge where his *hátei* (teacher) awaits. The young man feels the rich, soft earth beneath his bare feet. The Great Mother is supporting him. The greens, browns, and reds of the bushes and trees he passes are vibrant and alive, luscious in their exquisite beauty. The guardian spirits are present, reminding him of his people's heritage before recorded memory.

As he arrives at the ridge, he gasps. Before him stretches a vast expanse of mountains he has never seen, rising more than 18,000 feet from the Caribbean coast twenty-six miles away. The young man stands in awe. As much as anyone can, he is seeing the world for the first time. He has heard descriptions of it his whole life, but the outside world was only pictures in his imagination, like charcoal sketches without the explosion of color, sound, and scent that his senses now drink in.

For most of the past eighteen years, the young Arhuaco boy lived within the confines of the ceremonial men's circle that was his home, his school, and his temple. Arregoces, as we'll call him, lived in preparation for a sacred role in the tribe. His food was specially cooked for him, since all of it had to be white. From childhood he had been taught the intricacies of preparing the ceremonial elements and devotional offerings required for his sacred rituals. He learned to access *Se*, the spiritual core of existence in Arhuaco culture, and to interpret his visions, messages, and intuitions arising from *aluna*, the world of thought and imagination.

All of this had been carefully passed on by the tribal elders. Now Arregoces could traverse this mysterious inner realm with the skill of a trained explorer. Most important, he understood his role as one of the *Mamas*, "guardians of the world," who maintain balance and sustain life on Earth. The elders had shown him through repeated experiences that the true value in life arises from what lies beyond the senses, in the world of spirit. And now Arregoces was about to be "reborn" in the world, after finishing two intense periods of training, each lasting nine years and thus mirroring the nine months he spent in his mother's womb.

The hátei holds up a bowl of dried coca leaves. Arregoces places some in his mouth, chewing them into a soft ball that nestles against his cheek. (The leaves' effects are much milder than the concentrated cocaine extracted from them.) The hátei pours water into a gourd that contains roasted seashells gathered from the shore by an expedition of elders, and steam emerges. This results from a chemical reaction when the water mixes with the high concentration of lime in the seashells. The third element of his initiation, a pointed stick, is handed to him.

Arregoces puts the stick in his mouth and coats the pointed end with the wet coca, then inserts it into the steaming gourd. The lime-water reacts with the leaves, forming a yellowish substance, which he rubs along the round opening in the gourd. A deposit is left on the rim to dry into a crust, which he will add to, day after day, for the rest of his life. As it builds up into a thick layer, the sight will remind him of his duties as a spiritual guardian and sustainer.

The ritual we've described is a reconstruction based on the firsthand research of Dr. Wade Davis, the Explorer in Residence at the National Geographic Society, and Alan Ereira, an author and BBC reporter whose remarkable documentary, *From the Heart of the World* (www.thehiddenriches.com/heartoftheworld), was the tribes' first attempt to warn us, the "younger brothers," that we are destroying our planet.

The Arhuaco tribe lives in the northern mountains of Colombia, the Sierra Nevada de Santa Marta, and are remarkably unspoiled by the outside world. They are one of four tribes descended from Colombia's ancestral Tairona civilization, which was never conquered by the Spanish. When the conquistadors arrived, the chiefdoms retreated into the remote jungle mountains, where they lived, undisturbed by the vagaries of modern civilization, until the mid-1940s. Separated by language but united by spiritual beliefs and practices, three of the tribes, including the Arhuaco, have maintained their culture for at least a thousand years. Until recently they have refused to allow Westerners to enter their domain, except for a few very special exceptions.

Wade Davis has spent extensive time with the Arhuaco, first in the 1970s and again about thirty years later. He was one of the first outsiders allowed to observe the extraordinary coming-of-age ritual described in the story of Arregoces. Today his home in Washington, DC, serves as an unofficial embassy for the Arhuaco, who send delegations to us in an attempt to convey the urgency of our current global predicament.

The Arhuaco have directly experienced the devastating effects of global warming as the snowcaps on their sacred mountains have melted; the vegetation sustained by those snowcaps has died; and the violence surrounding the cocaine trafficking has decimated their people. As "elder brothers," they feel they have failed our world and now must come out to educate the "younger brothers" in the ways of spirit.

We began this book with a call to the world from one tribe, the Achuar, and end with another people who take responsibility for the state of nature and our place in it. Rituals meet a universal need for an orderly, peaceful, meaningful life. When you look around and see the threats that face our planet, you are hearing the world call out to you, and yet the voice is really your own. You are reconnecting to your sense of empathy, compassion, and human bonding.

One last ritual, then, to embrace everyone who has the intention of peace and the healing of our precious planet. It consists of a Vedic prayer whose words are ancient but whose intention is timeless:

> May the good belong to all the people in the world,
> May the rulers go by the path of justice.
> May the best of men and their source prove to be a blessing.
> May all the world rejoice in happiness.
> May rain come in time and plentifulness be on earth.
> May the world be free from suffering and the noble ones free
>   from fear.

Read this prayer and repeat it whenever you feel the world calling out to you, which could be every day. You won't help heal the world by worrying, suffering, getting depressed, or feeling helpless. You will help by strengthening your inner awareness. Your mission, if you choose to accept it, is reconnection. Inside your awareness exist all the tools to make it happen. Ritual is there to help your personal growth and to form visible bonds that reconnect all of us with one another. In this knowledge are tremendous hope and a reason to be optimistic. One person's Life Design expresses the design of life itself, which holds the answer to every problem.

APPENDIX

EASY REFERENCE GUIDE

For readers who want to quickly find a specific ritual, the guide below lists them by chapter. Most of these rituals appear in Part Two: Rituals to Meet Your Needs, but some are in other chapters. We encourage you to read the sections that lead up to each ritual—this will give you a fuller understanding of how that ritual will fulfill a need in your life.

We've also included the quizzes scattered throughout the book for easy reference.

A Vision of Fulfillment

Foundation Rituals

Your "Aha" Moment, and How to Get There

Rituals for Magical Relationships

Rituals for Diet, Health, and Beauty

The Art of Creating Wealth Through Ritual

Ceremonial Rituals and the Seasons of Life

Rituals for a Close Family Circle

How Dreams Come True

Expanding Your Awareness

NEXT STEPS

Discovering your Life's Design is a journey. It requires getting clear on who you are, what lights you up, and what gifts you've been born with. Whether this discovery process is new or old for you, you'll find proven tools and fun assessments to help you get clear on the unique design of your life and how to align with it at: www.thehiddenriches.com.

You probably know that change doesn't just happen. You've heard us say many times, "What you put your attention on grows stronger in your life." One of the great values of ritual is in helping you give attention to those things that will bring you more fulfillment.

And to get you started in discovering the transforming power of simple, easy-to-do, daily rituals, we designed the 30-Day Ritual Challenge—to help you make one significant change in your life to align with your passions and your unique purpose.

Enroll at: www.thehiddenriches.com/challenge.

We'll guide you through The Passion Test process to discover your top five passions, then we'll help you create a simple 5-minute ritual you can do each day to reinforce your intention for the change you are making. You'll be able to connect with others experiencing the same process through the Challenge Facebook group page.

Once you begin, every day you'll receive short video messages from us that will keep you inspired and guide you in creating a vision for your life along with an action plan for making it real.

Here's what a couple of participants had to say about the experience:

Thanks so very much for these 30 days. I was finally able to maintain a daily ritual!! I've been wanting to do this for years. Though I missed a couple of days (babysitting my 1 yr old granddaughter), the days before carried me thru—wow!! This has helped me refine/become more specific about what I want. Then things/opportunities started flying at me!! I'm just now catching my breath & getting used to this new whirlwind level of activity! I will joyfully continue my daily ritual—thanks again for the direction & support getting it going!! —Margaret Soloway

I want to thank you for such a powerful experience—'simple'? Very deceptive how this seemingly simple daily ritual is so empowering. I can identify daily actions and decisions that I chose in favor of my passions; if I wasn't doing the daily ritual, it would have been easy to veer off into 'practical' and 'have to'—those need to be done too, but passions first seems to give one energy. —Ildiko Haag

If you're ready to take what you've read and use it to change your life, the 30-Day Ritual Challenge is your ticket.

www.thehiddenriches.com/challenge

ACKNOWLEDGMENTS

From all of us: It's remarkable what a team effort it takes to create a book like this. We've been blessed with the support of an incredible team at Harmony Books, led by our amazing and remarkable editor, Mary Choteborsky. Thank you, Mary, for your clear guidance, your gentle nudging, your astute comments, and your wonderful flexibility.

Great thanks also goes to our publisher, Tina Constable, who remarkably was with us when we began the journey of becoming authors as we worked with her on the book of our dear friends, colleagues, and partners, Mark Victor Hansen and Robert Allen. Tina, thank you for your confidence in us and giving us the chance to work with your amazing team.

How do we thank the man who believed in us and pushed us to deliver our best? Scott Hoffman, you're our hero. Your brilliance astounds us, your heart touches us, and your friendship means everything to us. Having you as our literary agent has been one of our greatest blessings. And on top of all that, your karaoke is unmatchable.

If this book has any bits of brilliance and wisdom in it, it's because of the support and work of our dear friend and editor, George Brown. Through you and the inspired master that works through you, this book got done, and done well. We're so grateful.

Our sincere thanks goes also to the other members of our

Harmony team: Diana Baroni, Tammy Blake, Ellen Folan, Allison Judd, Meredith McGinnis, Christina Foxley, Derek Reed, and Stephanie Knapp.

Dean Draznin and the whole Draznin PR team, you rock! Thank you for getting this message out to the world in such a big way.

We conducted countless interviews with some of the world's most fun, interesting, and knowledgeable ritual experts. Our sincere thanks to all of you for taking the time when we know you didn't have much, and especially to Master Stephen Co, Dr. Alex Loyd, Dr. Andrew Newberg, Dr. Wade Davis, Lynne Twist, Dawn Gallagher, Rev. Michael Beckwith, Jack Canfield, Arielle Ford, Lynne McTaggert, and Dr. Eben Alexander.

When we went looking for the best examples of mandala art, the unseen forces of life led us to gifted Portuguese artist Joma Sipe. Joma, your generosity in sharing your gifts has touched our hearts deeply. We are honored and so grateful that you created the illuminated image of a fully expressed life on page 267 especially for this book. We sincerely hope that many of our readers will visit www.jomasipe.com and discover your beautiful art for themselves.

How would we have ever created this book without the inspiration and example of our dear sister, Marci Shimoff? Marci, you've been our rock, our guide, our support, and our greatest cheerleader. Your knowledge and brilliance when it comes to conveying a message is unmatchable. We love you so much!

Thank you dear Fairfield, Iowa (our very favorite vacation spot), for being so drenched in ritual that just being in this community is a constant reminder of what really matters in life.

Our deepest gratitude goes to the great teachers who opened our eyes and our hearts to the power of ritual and the unity of all things. For Janet and Chris, this was His Holiness Maharishi Mahesh Yogi.

No words can possibly express what we have gained from you. Our hope is that this book is a fitting offering to the blessings you have showered on us and on the world.

From Janet: Whew!! Well now comes the fun part. . . . To my dear angels, Suzanne Lawlor, Alexsandra Leslie, Dr. Sue Morter, Elisa Zinberg, and Marci, thank you so much for spending so much time thinking about this book with me during our Christmas holiday, giving me the best Christmas present of all—your pure genius.

To my buddy, Debra Poneman, thank you for your inspired feedback and your loving presence in my life.

To my precious assistant, Josephine, thank you for making sure the house was clean, the clothes were folded, flowers were everywhere, and my green drink was always there when I needed it as we immersed ourselves in creating this book.

To my brother, John, thank you for your invaluable, honest insights and feedback in reading the early drafts. And thank you to my sister, Mickey, for always checking in and loving me in the way only you can.

Dearest Sylva, thank you so much for getting as excited as I did about the possibilities of this book, so that I was inspired to actually sit down and start writing. Thank you for your amazing research that uncovered so many gems.

And Chris, thank you for realizing the potential that this book held and for being so completely, 100 percent focused on getting the book finished.

Lastly, thank you Bonnie Solow, our agent for *The Passion Test.* Your guidance as we created *The Passion Test* infused us with an impeccability, so much so that your wisdom was always with us as we created this new book.

From Chris: Wow! What a journey. How blessed I am to have the most loving, understanding, supportive, and nurturing wife. Doe, you are all that I dreamed of having as a life partner. Thank you for supporting me through the long days and long nights it took to get this done.

To Sophie Nandini Jyoti Bagambhrini Attwood, Tianna Satya Priya Devi Attwood, and Chetan Christopher Bala Rama Attwood, you are blessings from heaven for which I am so deeply grateful. Thank you for your patience and happy participation in our family rituals. Thank you for helping your daddy feel like the most fortunate man in the universe.

Dear sister Sylva, thank you for this amazing ride. Thank you for your patience, your love, and your brilliant contributions to making this book all that it can be. I'm thrilled that we got to do this together and am so excited to introduce you to the world!

Most especially, dear sister Janet (aka Janima), godmother to my children, my teacher, my guide, my business partner, and my best friend, thank you. Thank you for having the inspiration to bring this book into being and for allowing me to be a part of it. You've given me the chance to share my greatest passions and dive into the mystery of this wonderful experience we call life. I feel so deeply blessed to have you in my life.

From Sylva: I am in gratitude for this journey of ritual and birthing of this book. First, thank you to my parents. Without your tremendous courage to believe in freedom, I would never know the true meaning of the word. To all my family members, including my sister Radana, niece Anna, and nephew James, thank you for the life path we share.

Janet and Chris, you are part of my family, your presence in my life is a huge gift and blessing. My sister Janima, your passion and love reaches beyond this world. Brother Chris, your heart, deep kindness, and brilliance shines like the brightest star in the universe.

Travis, thank you for being my rock. You are solid in your presence, love, and support. I love you, my magnificent lion.

To my god-sisters, Mihaela, Jean, Sharon, Deborah, Stacie, and Kande, you and our many years of monthly ritual circle gatherings are a treasure in my life. Rosanne, thank you for your unwavering belief in me. To the many friends who supported me in birthing this book, including Liora, Annika, Agnes, Mark, Cristina, Phil, Leslie, Julie, Tami, Brian, Rose, Jana, John, Doe, and Rhya—thank you.

To all my teachers, mentors, and especially to His Divine Grace A.C. Bhaktivedanta Swami, thank you for your wisdom, your guidance, and your grace. To my clients, thank you, you inspire me. To my precious Angel, all the animal and nature spirits—daily you teach me the power in silence. Thank you.

I thank you God, knowing that through ritual we can experience creation and the sacred in every moment that makes everything possible! Amen.

Namaste.

INDEX

Wabi-sabi, 117, 118–119
Warehouse, mind as, 19–20, 32
Warren, Pastor Rick, 127, 128–133
The Way (film), 14–15
Weaknesses. *See* Problems/weaknesses
Wealth, creating, 146–171. *See also*
  Success
  about: overview of, 146–147
  "enlightened wealth" and, 5, 218, 268
  jar ritual, 167–171
  Mary Kay Ash (Mary Kay Cosmetics)
    and, 146, 147–148, 149, 150–153,
    154–155, 162
  Michelle's story, 167–171
  money, responsibility and, 148–149
  navigating crises and, 148
  objective measurement benefits,
    165–166

prosperity in various traditions and,
  251
service and, 166
tithing and, 170–171
transforming beliefs about money
  ritual, 157–160
value and, 166
Wisdom, world traditions and, 250
Women's/men's groups, 182
The Work (of Byron Katie), 230–
  235
World, predicament and ritual for
  healing, 271–273

Yao, Master, 80
You, "small" and "universal,"
  229